RELAUNCH!

5 Keys to Getting Past Stuck and Stress at Work and Life

Kim Hardy

DPMJ PUBLISHERS

RELAUNCH!
5 Keys to Getting Past Stuck and Stress at Work and Life

Copyright © 2014 by Kim Hardy

ISBN 0-9786187-5-0

To my husband, Dexter, who taught me how to dream big dreams. To my four precious jewels: Danielle, Philip, Monica and Jasmine... live the deepest dreams of your heart and never forget the Dream Giver. To Hope, GiGi loves you so much. Mom and Dad, thank you for teaching me how to use what I have and never give up. To Lisa, Ronald (Junior) and Craig, I'm so glad God blessed me to have you all as my siblings.

Contents

INTRODUCTION

During the process of writing this book, I attended a dinner party with a group of friends. While sitting around the table chatting and stuffing our faces, I shared the title of this book, *Relaunch: Five Keys to Getting Past Stuck and Stress at Work and Life.* And then I made the statement, "*So many people are stuck in life.*"

Before I could put my fork back in my mouth, my friend looked across the table at me and sincerely asked this question, "How do you know when you're stuck in life?"

Wow! This was my chance to share what I had learned through my research. But rather than giving her the neat and tidy, one-sentence philosophical answer that she probably expected, I spewed out an emotionally-charged sermonette. I was so passionate and fired up about the topic that I had a hard time stopping myself from downloading all the information inside me. Although they were my friends, I realized this was neither the time nor the place for my book debut.

But here's the thing. I'm passionate about helping people get past whatever is holding them back. I believe with everything in me that no one has to stay stuck or stressed out – especially when there are effective strategies to overcome it.

You see, I know what it feels like to be stressed out and stuck. And I know what it feels like to be free. I spent years—not days or months but years—in a state of stuck and under extreme stress. And now that I'm free, I'm taking my message to the world. I'm on a mission to help as many people as I can experience life in a whole new way.

So the next time someone asks me how do you know when you're stuck, I'll smile and hand them this book. A book packed with everything I wish I could have said that night.

STUCK AND BEING STRESSED WILL LOOK AND FEEL DIFFERENT FOR EVERYONE.

This is what I know about being stuck. Sometimes you are mentally clear enough to find just the right words to describe it. And then there are other times when there's nothing but raw emotions in your soul. Sometimes being stuck feels like you are at a crossroads between frustrated and furious. And sometimes you've settled into the notion that life is what it is. But one thing is for sure: You will flat out know when you are knee-deep in stuck.

I don't know what's keeping you stuck or stressed. But honestly, there are many ways people can find themselves in either situation.

You can be stuck or stressed because of:
- A lack of finances.
- A job you don't like.

- A relationship strain.
- A health concern.
- Worries about your future.

Whatever it is, no matter where you feel stuck or stressed, it bleeds into your entire life.

Listen, nobody likes being stuck or stressed, but it happens to all of us.

- Who hasn't wondered: Why am I still dealing with this same old stuff?
- Who hasn't thought: Why have I wasted my time on this?
- And who hasn't said: I've tried everything, and I don't see anything changing.

Take heart. The reason I wrote this book is to encourage you and to challenge you to not give up. You can relaunch again. You can have your own personal comeback story.

The key to getting past stuck and stress is to learn how to navigate the rough places with effective strategies so you don't have to stay there. Fortunately you've already started in the right direction by picking up this book. You're taking action and that's great. But relaunching and getting past stuck and being stressed-out is a process. And the first step in the process is what I call creating your own *personal growth path.*

Your personal growth path is a strategy or plan where you outline the action steps you're going to take to achieve the outcome you want in life. You may or may not have done anything like this before. But I can tell you from experience, when you design your growth path, and you become relentless in doing the small action steps daily, it will compound and you will begin to experience momentum. And that momentum will fuel your relaunch.

In this book I'm going to share strategies that can help position you for your best relaunch and help you navigate the challenges happening in your life.

Now please keep in mind, *this is not going to be an overnight process.* But you can be sure you can make progress. If you consistently live out your plan, you are going to see yourself moving toward your goals. That's what relaunching is all about.

In reality, we are never just stuck. We are either moving forward or backward. But not moving forward makes us feel stuck. So that's what we're going to call it.

I want you to know that I'm so excited for you. I know as you start moving in the direction you're aiming for, you'll quickly begin to experience momentum. There will be a newness and excitement in your life as you see yourself relaunching.

THE FIVE KEYS TO RELAUNCHING.

In this book, I will share the five keys that will help you develop and design your personal growth path.

The first key is: **DISCOVER THE ROOT CAUSE OF WHY YOU'RE STUCK.** This strategy will help you find out what is blocking your path.

The second key is: **RESHAPE YOUR THOUGHTS TO GET PAST STUCK.** Your thoughts take you either forward or backward. This strategy will help you combat negative thoughts.

The third key is: **UTILIZE THE RESOURCES YOU HAVE TO CREATE A RELAUNCH PLAN.** This strategy will help you to maximize the resources you have at your disposal to help you relaunch.

The fourth key is: **PREPARE FOR CRITICAL CONVERSATIONS TO JUMP-START YOUR JOURNEY.** This strategy will help you become more assertive when you need to confront certain people in your life.

The fifth key is: **CREATE HEALTHY OUTLETS TO LIFT YOUR STRESS AND KEEP YOUR SANITY.** This strategy will help you see the need to stop living beyond your capacity.

And finally, before we get started, I need to share two essentials to making these strategies work for you.

First, I want to challenge you not to hang your hopes on other people changing. The only person you can change is yourself. So focus all your energy on you and your personal growth path.

Second, it's important to capture your thoughts and emotions. So I have provided space for written responses that will help you process what is going on inside of you. Here's why I strongly encourage you to write a response to the questions.

The process of writing down your answers will:
- Help bring clarity out of your confusion.
- Help you explore new options and shift the way you think.
- Help you cement your commitment to change.

I know many of you may not like to write, but processing your thoughts by writing them down will become a powerful tool in your breakthrough.

Remember, this is a process and these strategies are to be adapted and modified to fit your particular situation. So use them to design your own personal growth path and get ready to relaunch!

WHEN THE THRILL IS GONE . . . AT WORK

Before the manuscript for this book was finished, I was asked to be on a radio show. As I expected, the host asked me about the subject matter of this book. What I didn't expect was the number of listeners who reached out to me after the program to pre-order the book and to share their stories.

Some stories were similar and some were different. But the common theme was that they were either stressed out about something going on at their job or they felt stuck where they were in life.

Let me quickly say, I can relate.

When I began relaunching my life, I was at a job I hated. And I know I'm not alone. As I've traveled in my speaking business, I've spoken to a lot of people who don't like their job or who feel stuck in it.

Why is that?

Well, think about it for a moment.

Remember when you first got the job you have now. Remember how excited you were the day you were hired. It may not have been an earthshaking moment, but more than likely you were thrilled. So thrilled that you called, emailed or texted your family and friends to share the good news. But now, with all the stress . . . THE THRILL IS PROBABLY GONE!

The thrill is so far removed that many employees can only think about that glorious day when they can walk into their boss's office and say those two sweet words... "I Q-U-I-T!"

Studies have revealed that a huge percentage of employees are disengaged, discouraged and ready to quit. Alarming? Maybe. But not that surprising.

Millions of people are going to work day after day stressed out and frustrated. Research reveals that many employees are fed up. They are downright sick of the crazy stuff that goes on at their job. Sick of the politics and unfair practices. Sick of being undervalued and underpaid. Sick of the demands and unrealistic expectations. And the number one thing disengaged employees say they are sick of is their boss.

Many employees are burned out, working below potential, and just trying to survive until something better comes along. There are countless thousands of people repeating the same routine job day after day without any real sense of meaning or purpose.

Think about it. That not only spells crisis in the workplace; that spells crisis in people's lives. And, unfortunately, most employees have no hope of anything changing for the better on their jobs. So they have mentally quit. In other words, millions of people in the world are functioning in a job where they have emotionally resigned. And studies have revealed that this employee disengagement is costing companies up to $550 billion a year. If that doesn't show that many people are stuck and stressed, I don't know what does.

Perhaps that's why author Daniel Goleman, widely known for his book *Emotional Intelligence,* says, "…the time for ignoring emotions as irrelevant to business has passed."

I believe it's time we take a hard look at our emotions. Why? Although emotions alone should never guide our lives, we have emotions for a reason. When we find ourselves emotionally down more than we are emotionally up, it's a sign that something needs to change.

Your emotions can be an indicator that you need to take action. Wise action. Your present struggle can be the drive you need to do what you probably should have done a long time ago. And that is to take the necessary steps to improve your life. Unfortunately, most people won't make needed changes until something rocks their world. That's what happened to me.

Honestly, I can now thank God for my terrible job situation. Before you think I'm sick in the head, hear me out.

Without my job challenge, I would have never positioned myself to make the progress I've made in my life. My miserable job was a catalyst to my breakthrough. My job caused me to think deeper about my life and what I really wanted. It was during that time I realized I wanted to be an author and professional speaker. And now I have gone on to expand my business into coaching and consulting individuals and organizations. All of that came out of my life mess.

If all of that can happen for me, what can happen for you?

Consider this thought. Your job, or whatever challenge you're facing, can actually be the catalyst to help you get the breakthrough you need.

This can be huge for you.

This can be your defining moment.

And hopefully as you read this book you'll begin to visualize your buffet of options and possibilities that already surround you.

So now we'll look at the process of getting past stuck and how you can relaunch right where you are.

YOU CAN RELAUNCH RIGHT WHERE YOU ARE

In the introduction I shared with you how I was stuck for years and how passionate I have become in my pursuit to help other people get unstuck. I'll be sharing more details of my story throughout the book. But for now, let me share the situation that rocked my world and left me wondering if I would ever recover.

My story's not tragic like many stories I've heard over the years. But it is tragic in that I stopped living life. My painful story was my *dark night of the soul*. And during that period, I didn't appreciate the value of life or time. I wasted precious moments living in emotional agony with no real plan and no hope of things changing. And unfortunately I settled in the state of being stuck.

Here is the short version of my long story.

I grew up in a small, working-class town in Ohio. It was a great place to raise children back in the late sixties and seventies. Although I come from a family with humble roots, I always felt secure. In my early childhood, my father made a low middle-class salary and, unfortunately, we lived from paycheck to paycheck. I know most of you are thinking—join the crowd!

Unfortunately, my father's steel mill employer closed down in the late seventies. But despite our financial limitations, my parents were determined to make the most out of our situation. Although money was scarce, my parents taught my siblings and me that one way to survive was to start your own business. So as a young teen I can remember selling suckers to my classmates, trying to figure out ways to market them and make a profit.

Eventually I put the entrepreneurial bug to the side, but it was always in my blood. And my mom and dad continued to trudge through business after business until all the money dried up.

After I reached adulthood, I left my hometown behind and married the man of my dreams. We moved to the big state of Texas and settled in the suburbs of Dallas so my husband could pursue a graduate degree.

After he graduated, we moved back to Columbus, Ohio, about three hours from my hometown. By this time we had acquired two children and lots of bills. So to help with our tight budget, I decided the best thing to do was to fall back on what I knew as a child. Start a business.

I remember the day like it was yesterday when I got the idea to start my own business. I shared this great idea with my husband, but he wasn't sure it was the right thing for us to do at the time. Well, with my background, it made perfect sense. Although we didn't have actual money, we had the credit that would allow us to borrow the money. Reluctantly my husband got on board. But by that time I was already planning away.

I had consulted with my family back home on the idea. I thought it was best to start the business in my hometown, because there I would have help running the day-to-day operations. Within six months, my business was up and running.

My business was a resell shop. And many of the items we sold were returns from major department stores. My job was to find these lots of items, which cost thousands of dollars, and then resell them at a markup.

Unfortunately, the business began going south after a year. And I spent the next few years trying to save it. I eventually moved my sister into a partnership role, which caused more problems than it solved. She quickly restructured the business and went full force with her agenda. We had intense conversations daily, and although I was ticked off most days, I understood that it was her cash and her ideas that were keeping us afloat.

While trying to save the business, we used various marketing approaches: direct mail, radio and television commercials, and even putting balloons on signs. We were in search of quick fixes. And since we were in crisis mode, we didn't have time to critically think or reflect on what was working and what wasn't. We were just trying to put a band-aid on a sinking ship.

I knew we were in financial trouble. And it was an inescapable reality that we were going to go out of business soon. But the day it happened was one of the hardest days of my life. When I came to my place of business and found they had locked the doors because we hadn't paid the rent, my heart sank.

I officially felt like a failure. My attempt at business had failed. And my life's dream disappeared before my eyes.

Even though the writing had been on the wall, I never thought this day would come. I felt my business would somehow survive. Even on the difficult days, I had fought hard to shrug off any thoughts of closing the doors. I didn't realize that my passion to keep the business open was going to cost me emotionally, spiritually, and psychologically—not to mention financially.

Over the course of the life of that business, I drained every penny we had to keep it going. I focused all my energy on keeping the doors opened. I desperately needed that business to succeed. And I desperately needed to see my dream of being an entrepreneur come true.

Now that the doors were closed, what was I going to do? I had no fallback plan of doing anything else. Earlier in my life I tried working a normal 9-to-5 job, but it never worked for me. When I tried it, I honestly felt like I was being suffocated. I thought it was going to literally kill me. It was so out of alignment with who I was as a person.

My interest and passion had always been to own and operate my own business. That's all I knew, and that was all I could see.

So when my business was forced to close, I didn't know what to do. I was emotionally crippled.

For years I lived in a state of stuck. I lived in depression. And sadly, my husband and children had to live with me in that state.

Fortunately, I was functionally depressed. And thankfully I was able to get a job. But I hated it. As I reflect back on that situation, I realize that it really didn't matter what the job was, I was a misfit for it.

As a depressed person, I lived in my past. I lived in my failure. And I replayed that defeated script over and over again in my head. I constantly thought about the significant financial loss and how my choices adversely affected my family. It was hard to forget, especially since the bill collectors wouldn't let me. They must have had my number on speed dial.

My days were filled with regret and self-pity. And all I thought about was everything I had wasted. All my money, time, and energy—on a failed dream. I couldn't let it go. I was stuck right there.

But one day I made the decision that I didn't want to be miserable any longer. And like many of you reading this book, I couldn't leave my job. But things had to change or I was going to lose it. That was the day I learned a valuable principle: *You can relaunch right where you are.*

I determined in my depression that my dreams were not over. I just needed to heal and to develop my character. I needed to heal so I could live again and dream again. My dreams needed to be *repurposed, reshaped and relaunched.* And my character needed to be more aligned with my faith and my core values.

Here's what I know: Becoming unstuck starts in the mind. It begins with rethinking everything. And embracing the fact that you are not without choices. If nothing else, you get to choose how you will look at life. I realized I had a choice and I was not going to stay stuck in my emotional state any longer. I became relentless in seeking a change in my life.

With God's help, I began to take a proactive role in my life, utilizing timeless truths and using creative strategies and tools to get past stuck.

Although I didn't become unstuck overnight, I quickly began to see noticeable results in my personal and professional life that allowed me to experience what I call a *relaunch.* And it's that process I'm going to share with you in this book.

KEY# 1
DISCOVER THE ROOT
CAUSE OF WHY
YOU'RE STUCK

"We should not look back unless it is to derive useful lessons from past errors, and for the purpose of profiting by dearly bought experience."

- George Washington

THE POWER OF REFLECTION.

My life before my great relaunch looked similar to this: Every day I had two realities that collided. I was stuck in my past business failure and I was stuck in my present job situation. I was stressed out and I hated where I was in life. And, unfortunately, my family bore the brunt of my frustration. It was normal for me to be cranky with my children and agitated with my husband. I was on edge about everything. So believe me when I tell you I was the Queen of Stuck.

I found myself in between not wanting to live and not wanting to die. I was stuck right there.

It was a sad way to live to be sure. But fortunately, even in my depression, I began my relaunch. It began when I recognized I needed to quit looking just at the symptoms of my challenges and struggles, and start looking at the root cause of how I became stuck. I needed to look not only at the external factors like my job dissatisfaction and my business failure, but also at internal factors that had contributed to my becoming stuck.

It was in reflecting that I uncovered things about me that I'd never recognized before. Things you will hear about in upcoming pages.

But for now, let me challenge you to apply the power of reflection. Here's why. When you're stuck, something has stopped working for your benefit. And you need to know what that something is. Because that will tell you what adjustments and changes you need to make.

So everything in your life needs to go under the microscope...including you. As you delve into your life, you'll begin to see issues come to the surface. Issue that you may have never realized the impact they had on you.

Think of it this way: You must become like a detective who takes apart the scene of a crime. Why? Because he understands that he has a better chance of solving the crime not by just looking at the obvious, but also by looking at the most subtle clues. A good detective will leave no rock unturned. So I want you to look under every rock in your life.

You must be willing to invest time in personal excavating. In other words, you'll have to interrogate and examine everything about yourself. You'll need to look at your assumptions and your beliefs. You'll have to observe your thoughts, your behaviors, your patterns and your emotions. You'll need to look at the decisions you've made and discover why you made them. You'll need to look at the people you have allowed into your life and why you let them in.

Being stuck is a sign that something along your path didn't work. Now it's time for a change. It's time for better choices.

As you step back and reflect on when, where and how you became stuck, you'll be able to make better sense of your life and figure out what you need to do to start moving forward. You'll gain more clarity and become wiser as you look back for analysis.

It's important to keep exploring. Keep looking to find answers. Because when you do find the answers, the insights will help you in two ways.

First, you'll become acutely aware of the ways you may be stuck or stressed. Second, you'll learn effective ways of getting past stuck and being stressed and preventing it in the future.

The more exploring you do, the more answers you'll find to help you design your growth path and make your great relaunch.

DO YOU KNOW WHAT'S HOLDING YOU BACK?

Two days ago I was on the phone with a coaching client, listening to him share about the frustrations he was having on his job. At the beginning of the conversation all he could talk about was how his job was a stumbling block for him. But as I helped him to dissect his life by reflecting on certain factors, he discovered there was more holding him back than just his job. He discovered these truths by taking the time to reflect and look deeper into his life. Now he is able to focus on his growth path with an honest and realistic assessment of what he needs to do.

Like my client, there's something blocking your path. So tell me, what is getting in your way? What is keeping you stuck or stressed?

You may be able to answer this question quickly, or maybe not. But think on that question for a moment.

I know it might sound like a simple question at first. And you may be able to quickly rattle off some reasons why you became stuck. But what if there were more reasons than you realized? I'm sure you would want to know what they are.

I don't expect you to come away with all the answers, but this is a great starting point. It will require some time, so don't rush it. It's best to take some time out by yourself—even if it's only fifteen minutes a day over several weeks. However you choose to do it, make the minutes count by removing all the distractions you can so you can think.

For some people, a time of reflection needs to begin with prayer and meditation. That's how I like to start. For others, a nice walk in the park may help you think more clearly about past events. And for some, creating a quiet place in your favorite room in the house and sipping on a good cup of coffee helps you relax and think. Whatever helps you position your mind so that you can rewind is what you need to do to get started. And then ask yourself a ton of questions. Questions like:

- How long have I been upset about this particular issue?
- Why have I allowed this issue to go on for so long?
- How does this challenge or situation affect my outlook on my future?

Whatever questions you ask of yourself, be sure to ask open-ended questions. And as you ask yourself questions, think of this process as a learning opportunity. An opportunity to position yourself for your great relaunch.

Please don't skip this critical part of reflecting and asking questions. I know that looking back is not something you probably want to do. But if your goal is to get unstuck, reflection will reveal many needed answers. And when you get past stuck, reflection should be part of your ongoing process.

As you go through the reflection process, eventually you'll gain understanding and clarity as to exactly how you traveled to the world of stuck and stress. So keep unrolling your life until you discover how you got to this emotional place. Don't get frustrated at what you find. Stick to the process.

If you're stuck or stressed, there are things in your life holding you back. I call them "barriers to relaunch."

The greatest threat to your relaunch may be some of the barriers listed below. My friend, you need to be aware of any barriers that are impeding your growth path. The list below is not all encompassing, so feel free to add some of your own to it.

HOW MUCH OF A ROLE IS *BLAME* PLAYING IN YOUR LIFE?

"My supervisor is so incompetent. No wonder I can't get my job done."

There have been times in my life when I have surrendered to blame. And yes, there were times I felt justified in blaming other people. Even as I'm writing, I can recall a time when I was passed over for a promotion that everyone knew I deserved. But because of office politics, I didn't get it.

I can also think of a time when a family member made a crushing comment about me that wasn't true. Although he apologized, the damage was already done. And whoever said words don't hurt, needs to be slapped with a couple of them. Words do hurt and words can cause damage.

The truth is: Life is not easy for you and it isn't easy for me.

And, unfortunately, life sometimes has to beat us up before we wake up.

In the past I allowed blame to hold me back and shackle my dreams and desires. But, thank goodness I woke up to the fact that blame was not benefiting my life. And now those days are gone.

I am convinced that nobody has the power to hold me back but me.

So my friend, if you want to get out of stuck or not get stressed out, make sure you don't lock yourself up in the prison of blame.

Here's the big challenge for you. Tremendous growth takes place as you accept responsibility for your part in your life circumstances.

I'm reminded of the story of Adam and Eve. Adam and Eve were in a perfect environment called Eden. And all God required of them was to obey him. Part of their obedience meant they were not to eat from the tree of the knowledge of good and evil. But eventually a serpent enticed Eve to eat. Eve gave in to the serpent and then invited Adam to eat. After Adam ate, they soon realized they were naked and began to find leaves to cover up.

When God came to visit them in the Garden, it was accountability time. But no one wanted to take responsibility for their actions. Instead of owning up to what they had done, Adam and Eve passed the blame around. They were looking for scapegoats. Adam blamed God for giving him Eve. Eve blamed the serpent. And the blame game continues on to this day.

Think about how many people have blamed you for something. And how many people have you blamed for something?

Whether we admit it or not, there is temptation to blame our situation on someone or something other than ourselves. I guess it's always easier to pass the blame than own up to our part in a situation.

Even if a person has wronged you or betrayed you, they're probably not going to own up to their part. So your next step is to let go of the pain that person has caused you. Now you may have to go through counseling to get over this hurdle. But do whatever is necessary so you can make your great relaunch.

Remember, blame can't help you. Accountability and responsibility can. I love this quote by Jim Rohn: "You must take personal responsibility. You cannot change the circumstances, the seasons, or the wind, but you can change yourself."

Where has blame become a part of your life? Use the following space to unload your thoughts.

____

____

____

____

____

____

____

HOW MUCH TIME DO YOU SPEND IN *SELF-PITY*?

As a mother of four, I have heard every one of my children make this statement: *"It's not fair."* And every time they made that statement, I would say the same phrase (and you have probably said it, too), *"Life isn't fair."*

It's funny now to think about it, but after my business failure I never uttered the words *it's not fair.* But that's how I lived my life. I felt sorry for myself. I felt sorry that I was broke and I had to take a job that I didn't like, and work for a company that I didn't like, and live in a home I didn't like, and drive a car I didn't like. And in the end, I realized *I didn't even like me.*

I know that sounds terrible. But remember this: Self-pity never looks good on anyone. And self-pity never helps you rise up. Instead it always takes you down.

I know I'm not the only adult that has ever embraced self-pity. I'm sure you've done it, too.

The truth is we've all attended the "woe is me" party a few times.

- Why did this happen to me?
- What did I do to deserve this?
- How come no one understands me?

Just the other day, my husband met a man who had just been laid off. So when I met him, I could tell he was drenched in self-pity. He was as cold as a fish. You could see it all over his face. He was mad at the world and pouting like a baby. And yet he didn't even realize it.

Here's a sobering thought: Wallowing in self-pity keeps you in the waiting line. It keeps you dependent on someone else. Who wants to wait for someone else to come to your rescue and save you from your problems? Most of the time no one shows up. And if they do, they're usually a little too late.

I share my story because the truth is life will sometimes kick us in the butt and leave us wounded. But your empowerment happens when you decide not to stay wounded. Your empowerment happens when you determine to get up and not stay down.

The choice is yours. It's all about how you respond. I say, when you get down, it's time to rebound. It's time to relaunch. This is your life. Don't waste another minute of it in self-pity.

Can you identify any self-pity in your life? If so, describe it in the following space.

____

____

____

____

____

____

____

____

____

HOW MANY OF YOUR THOUGHTS
ARE FILLED WITH *REGRET*?

Every time I had to talk to a bill collector on the phone to try to negotiate a payment plan for all the bills from my business, I regretted the fact that I had even started that business. I regretted all the times I was not honest with my husband about the financial shape the business left us in. I regretted that I didn't position myself to be able to get a better job once the business closed.

I regretted so much that it led me straight into depression.

After years of being swallowed up in regret, I decided it was time to take action. The regret was leading me nowhere but deeper into the pits.

If you're going to get past stuck and stress, you're going to need to have closure with all your regrets. Yes, you may have made some wrong choices, decisions, and mistakes. Who hasn't? And yes, you've dealt with some level of consequences. But regret will keep you from relaunching.

How much time have you spent regretting a particular choice or situation? When was the last time you thought about what you woulda, coulda or shoulda done? And what payoff did you get from that kind of thinking?

The challenge before you is not to get stuck in the web of regret. If you don't deal with regrets, they build up until you begin to fall apart.

Once I realized regret was a barrier in my life, I responded with strategic action.

1 I asked God for forgiveness for all of my wrong actions.

2 I then asked my husband for forgiveness.

3 And then, the hardest part of all, I decided to forgive myself.

And finally, with forgiveness in hand, I took the actions I describe in this book to move my life forward. Now I will never pretend that it was easy. But it was easier with a strategic plan.

I tell you my story because I want you to know not only the destructive power of living in regret, but also the healing power of forgiveness.

So if you have done something wrong, take the needed steps to make it right. Don't torture yourself.

Use regret as:

A reminder that everyone makes mistakes. Use your mistakes as a motivator to reach your new goals.

A teaching tool. Extract every ounce of wisdom you can from your experience and allow the lessons to launch you forward.

Now it's your turn to share.

What have you regretted lately and what are you going to do about it?

____

____

____

____

____

HOW IS *UNFORGIVENESS* PREVENTING YOUR RELAUNCH?

I briefly mention forgiving myself and asking forgiveness of others. But what about extending forgiveness to another person? Now that's a biggie, I know. And I'm sure you know it's not easy to forgive. Especially if you've been hurt deeply by someone you trusted.

Please understand, forgiving someone is a process. But don't wait on your feelings to catch up to the process. Your feelings may never come. But you still need to forgive. Why? Because unforgiveness locks you in an emotional prison and prevents you from living your life to its fullest.

Whenever I've gotten to the point where I realize I'm withholding forgiveness, I remember how much God and others have forgiven me. I also pray for the power to be able to release myself and that person from the pain they have caused me.

As you know, one small section on the subject of forgiveness is not nearly enough to do justice to the topic. So if you need to, please seek out help. There are spiritual and professional counselors who specialize in wounds of the heart and can help you begin your healing process.

Here is a quote I came by the other day by Tyler Perry that really sums up what I hope you will embrace: "When you haven't forgiven those who've hurt you, you turn back against your future. When you do forgive, you start walking forward."

My friend, this is your time to move forward. So determine today not to allow unforgiveness to be a barrier in your life.

Is there anyone you need to forgive? If so, what will be your next steps in beginning the process?

____

____

____

____

____

HOW IS *FEAR* HOLDING YOU BACK?

What is that one fear that seems to keep rising up in your life? I have mine and I know you have yours. Whatever it is, I am convinced that we can fight it.

I just read a part of a book title on how to deal with fear. It said: *PUNCH IT IN THE FACE.* I just love that statement. I wish I could claim it as mine. I saw those words on the cover of author Jon Acuff's latest book, *Start: Punch Fear in the Face, Escape Average and Do Work that Matters.* And I thought . . . yes, that's how you do it! Sucker punch fear in the face and keep on moving.

A nicer way to say it comes from Dale Carnegie, author and lecturer, who said: "Do the thing you fear to do and keep on doing it . . . that is the quickest and surest way ever yet discovered to conquer fear."

We all have fears:

- Fear of change
- Fear of failure
- Fear of rejection
- Fear of commitment

If your fear isn't listed, it's because there are too many to write down. But you get the point.

Let me ask you a few questions for deep, reflective thought.

1   What do you really want to do in life but your fear keeps holding you back?

2   How has fear robbed you of something you've dreamed of?

3   What limitations have you placed on yourself because of fear?

4   How much of what you fear has come true?

My friend, I want you to write your answers to those four questions in the space below. But before you get started, I want you to finish reading this section.

Remember this: ***Fear will always rob you of something you really want.***

I remember the day our son celebrated his third birthday with a party. All week long he was so excited about having his friends come over to the house to celebrate his special day. Even though he was only turning three, he knew this day was all about him. He knew he was going to be in the spotlight and he was ready for it. He knew every gift had his name on it and he was prepared to open them. He was so excited the day of the party— until he saw the clown.

He wasn't aware we had decided a clown would be a great addition to the party.

Much to our surprise, our son was scared to death of the clown costume. He was so terrified that he ran like a crazy person to his room and hid under his bed. As hard as we tried to convince him to come out, it didn't work. We even revealed to him who the clown was. It was his Dad.

But by this time, it didn't matter. Fear had gripped his heart

I can remember squatting down looking under the bed at his cute little chubby face. Nothing we said calmed his fear. Even though we told him that all of his friends were eating his birthday cake and ice cream, it didn't make any difference. He still isolated and insulated himself under the bed, nestled in his own fear. He actually thought he was safe and secure and free under his bed. But in reality he was trapped. If he had chosen to come out from under the bed, he would have enjoyed real freedom. The freedom of being with his friends and eating his own birthday cake. He allowed his fear to rob him of the one special day of the year where all the gifts, well wishes and love were showered on him.

I share that story because that is what happens to you and me when we allow fear to make our decisions. Fear blocks us from experiencing so much opportunity to enjoy a greater life. Fear causes us to create our own insulating methods. And in reality, much of what we fear never comes true. And even if a small percentage of what we fear comes true, it doesn't destroy us.

You are the owner of your fear and you can fight it. You conquer fear not by denying its presence, but by:

- Acknowledging your fear.
- Focusing and fighting for the outcome you really desire.
- Recognizing that truth is a great weapon against fear.
- Reminding yourself that on the other side of your fear is freedom.
- Daily doing at least one thing that you fear.
- Celebrating as you take steps past fear.

If you want to get past fear, take steps one day at a time until you find that you have crossed your threshold. And only you know where your threshold of fear is. As you do one thing a day to conquer your fear, your confidence will build. But don't forget, fear won't go away without you punching it in the face with relentless action.

Start taking action by answering the questions I listed above.

____

____

____

____

____

____

____

____

HOW IS *SELF-DOUBT* SABOTAGING YOUR LIFE?

When I was starting my speaking business, I had to fight all kinds of doubt that began to creep into my mind. Thoughts like:

- Who will listen to you?
- What makes you a professional?
- What if you fail at this too?

Why do we fall into the trap of thinking less of ourselves? I'm not going to say I no longer battle self-doubt or low self- confidence, because I'd be lying. But I have learned how to fight it. I am convinced that one of the greatest struggles most of us have is our self-doubt. I used to think I was by myself until I began to have honest conversations with other people. I have talked to countless people through the years and learned that self-doubt is a personal struggle many people face.

Frankly, we can be our own worst enemy. We think such negative thoughts about ourselves. When was the last time you wanted to try something bold or new? How long was it before self-doubt crept in?

When was the last time you thought:

- What a stupid idea.
- Who am I to try to do that?
- Somebody else will probably win the bid instead of me.

Think about it. We are the ones who ultimately place limitations on ourselves. We are the ones that program our thoughts to see the negative about ourselves. We are the ones that replay our past failures in our head.

And many times we are unaware of the magnitude of the impact self-doubt is having on us. We can be very critical of ourselves and not even realize it.

In reflecting, have you recognized that sometimes you can be your harshest critic and how much negative self-talk has played a role in your being stuck? Have you realized that self-doubt is actually self-rejection?

It is vitally important to detect the signs of self-doubt and take action immediately, before it does any more harm. Try some of these ideas:

Make bold affirmations. True affirmations tear down any lies that you may be thinking. I love to quote a verse I found in the Bible that says with God all things are possible. So whenever I come up against a challenge, I quote that verse. I know that with God there is nothing I cannot do that I am created to do. I put the spotlight on that truth. I live in that truth. And I speak that truth in my life. What's a bold affirmation you can say to yourself?

Focus on facts rather than just feelings. Sometimes we feel unworthy. And sometimes we may feel insecure about who we are. Clearly we all have flaws. But recognizing flaws and tearing yourself down are two totally different things.

When I'm beating myself up or allowing insecurity to rise up, I remind myself that I may not be good at everything, but I am good at some things—and many times even great at what I do. I am able to determine this by the fact that thousands of people have affirmed the quality of my gifts and talents. Who am I to rip myself apart? I have made a commitment to myself to fight self-doubt. I won't sabotage myself. How about you? Will you make a commitment to not stand in your own way with self-doubt?

Have an accountability plan in place. One way I fight self-doubt is by telling my trusted friends to kick me in the butt when they see that I am giving in to self-defeating behavior. I have given them permission to speak truth into my life. They not only challenge me, but they remind me of my mission in life and the goals I have to make a difference in the world.

Finally, a word of warning: Don't allow self-doubt to hold you back from relaunching. Recognize it when it comes and confront it with action steps. One huge step would be to find someone to hold you accountable to staying on your growth path.

Now let me ask you: What part is self-doubt playing in your life right now?

____

____

____

____

____

ARE YOU READY TO MOVE FORWARD?

Now that you have reflected and have a greater awareness of some of the barriers that may have been blocking

your path, hopefully you feel the door to progress beginning to open.

Imagine what your future life could look like uncon-
taminated by any of these barriers. It really boils down
to a change in thinking and a change in choices. So in
the chapter ahead, let's look at how you can reshape your
thinking for your relaunch. It's time to develop rigorous
and relentless thinking to stay on course.

KEY# 2
RESHAPE YOUR THOUGHTS TO GET PAST STUCK

"We can not solve our problems with the same level of thinking that created them."

- Albert Einstein

YOU ARE NOT ALONE.

"I am completely burned out."
"I want out of my job, but where else can I go?"
"I have very little family support."
"I have gotten to the point where I cry almost every day."
"I am so stressed out."
"I don't know what I really want out of life."
"I feel like I'm wasting my time at this job."

UNSHACKLE YOUR THOUGHTS.

With everything that is going on in your life right now, it's probably hard to stay positive. Especially if you're in an environment surrounded by negative people. I'll be honest with you. It's going to be a fight to keep your thoughts focused and not get sidetracked. But it's a fight you can win. I wrote this chapter to give you some tools that will help.

First let me ask you a question: How many negative phrases have you thought or said today?

I asked that question for a reason. It took me most of my life to learn this simple yet complex truth—my thoughts have the power to take me up or bring me down.

It took my depression for me to see the destructive damage of nurturing the wrong kind of thoughts. As I look back on my journey, I realize I was mentally malnourished. My thoughts were definitely unhealthy.

I remember waking up in the morning with dreaded thoughts of going to work. I hated my job and the last thing I wanted to do was act giddy and positive. Not only did I hate my job, I hated the commute there. So my morning drive was filled with complaining. If there was rain, snow, or sun, I found something to complain about. It was either too hot, too cold, or too wet.

And it didn't stop there. I complained about the rising price of gas and the stupid orange construction cones. And my worst complaint was about the idiot drivers that were on the road every morning.

You may be wondering why I didn't get psychological help. Well that was my other complaint. I couldn't afford it. I warned you earlier that I was the Queen of Stuck. I bet you believe me now.

I allowed my circumstances and my challenges to shape my thoughts and determine my outlook on life. And now that I think about it, I even allowed other people—people who were stuck themselves—to influence my thoughts. That's ridiculous and even funny to me now.

Studies say that we have at least 70,000 thoughts a day. That's a whole lot of thoughts. And when you feel stuck, a lot of what you're thinking is not positive, uplifting, you-can-do-it kind of thoughts.

When you are trying to relaunch, you need as many positive and factual thoughts as possible. Just observe how you feel after thinking a positive versus a negative thought. Look at the difference in your emotions.

According to Harvard researcher Shawn Achor, author of The Happiness Advantage, "When we are positive, our brains become more engaged, creative, motivated, energetic, resilient, and productive…"

Researcher Barbara Fredrickson says positive emotions *broaden* your sense of possibilities and open your mind, which in turn allows you to *build* new skills and resources that can provide value in other areas of your life.

Hmmm. Reading that tells me we need to get to work on our thoughts. So how do we start?

BE ON THE ALERT FOR NEGATIVE THINKING.

"I'm never going to get out of this mess."
"I'm sick of living like this. Nothing is going to change."
"I should be at a certain point by now."

Can you relate to any of those thoughts? I can because they were mine when I was going through my depression. Of course those thoughts didn't serve me well. That's why I intentionally began to change what I was thinking.

One of the prevailing thoughts in my mind during my depression was, *"I should be further along in life by now."*

Here's the thing. Although that was an accurate assessment of my life, I didn't have to take a negative spin on it. What I eventually did was start my relaunch plan by being on the lookout for negative thoughts. I began to focus on where I wanted to go and how I was going to get there. I chose to counter my negative thoughts with positive ways of how I was going to reach my goals. Eventually my thoughts began to fill up with all the possibilities ahead of me. Why? Because I made a plan and I was determined to line up my thoughts with that plan.

Now let me ask you. What thoughts are you thinking that are bringing you down?

My friend, please hear me. If you want a different life, you are going to have to change your thinking patterns. You're going to have to start thinking in a way that will bring you up and not drag you down. I'm not saying you should deny reality, but you can extract positive even out of a negative situation.

ELEVATE YOUR THOUGHTS.

My daughter's wallet was stolen a few days ago and she was rightfully upset. But after I allowed her to process her anger, I helped her extract the positive out of that negative situation. I asked how much money she had in her wallet. She told me she had twenty-five dollars in it. I then said, "The good news is it wasn't as much as you usually would have had in your wallet."

Do you see where I'm going with this? You can always elevate your thoughts when you intentionally extract the positive out of the negative.

I didn't dismiss the value of the money, her loss, or her emotions. However I did want her to see that it could have been worse. She could have been attacked or killed for her wallet. But she wasn't.

Her wallet was stolen after she accidently dropped it in a restaurant. When she went back to get it, it was gone. I guess the thief thought it was a gift. Yes it was a big inconvenience to cancel her credit cards and replace her license. But I helped her elevate her thoughts by focusing on the fact that she had the ability to replace things, but she couldn't replace a life.

Listen to this quote I came across the other day by Norman Vincent Peale, "Change your thoughts and you change your world."

I agree.

If your current thoughts are not taking you where you want to go, *change them.*

Do you really want to get unstuck? Then be prepared to replace your negative thoughts. Learn the strategy of exchanging a thought for a thought.

When a thought is not benefiting you, confront that thought and replace it with one filled with possibility, that's factual, and that is also inspiring—and think that thought. Why? Because this is a huge part of relaunching. There are opportunities awaiting you, and you need to be mentally prepared to seize them.

Whatever is consuming your thoughts, ask yourself if it's adding to your growth or restricting it. Think of one positive thought that you can use to replace a negative thought you might be thinking. Try using this strategy and see the difference it will make. You'll be armed and ready when the conversation in your head is not going in the direction you want it to.

Now to your situation. How can you elevate your thoughts?

I know this might be hard, but no one ever said life would be easy. The reason you have to elevate your thoughts is because it's essential to the quality of your life. Yes you may be going through a difficult time, but you can still find something positive.

Just try it. Take some time to write down something you don't like about your situation and then write two positive views you can extract out of it. As you do this, think about how you can include this strategy in your life on a regular basis. Establish a mental trigger to remind you to extract the positive out of any adverse situation.

____

____

____

____

____

____

____

TALK BACK TO YOUR THOUGHTS.

Talking to yourself does not mean you're crazy. A part of how I came through my depression was by talking to myself—out loud. I would say, "I might be down, but this will pass." I said that to myself because I wasn't going to feed the darkness in my soul anymore. I refused to take a laidback approach and give in to my emotions, even when I felt my life was hanging on by a thread. Tears and all, I took action with my words. I learned how to think positively and talk positively to myself.

- What powerful words can you say to encourage yourself on your journey?
- What powerful statements can you say to yourself to keep your thoughts focused?

Here is some space to write down what you can say to encourage yourself.

____

____

____

____

____

____

____

ADD GRATITUDE TO THE MIX.

I'm not sure of the precise moment I began to have a new perspective about my life, but I remember the role gratitude played in helping to reshape my thoughts and get me past stuck. Gratitude is such a powerful tool that I still use it in my life daily.

Being grateful helps me put things in perspective. Gratitude says I refuse to focus on all the things I don't have when I have so much to be thankful for.

Whenever I begin to whine or complain, I know I'm not in a state of gratitude.

No matter what's going on in my life, it could always be worse. So when I do begin to whine, I have some reminders to help me snap back into gratefulness.

One of those reminders is a friend who has a debilitating disease. She wasn't born with this illness, and she wasn't aware of anything until symptoms of this disease began to show up on her wedding day.

And since that day, her life has never been the same.

I met her for the first time at a conference. I observed her as she maneuvered her way around the crowded room with the assistance of a cane and a smile. Her radiance eventually walked toward me and we immediately struck up a conversation. We discovered we had a lot in common and decided to exchange phone numbers. It took a while before we connected again, but as we talked I got to hear more of her story. And over the years, her story and her life have changed.

She no longer walks on her own. She is totally wheelchair-bound and needs the help of others to do the simplest tasks. She cannot cut up her food and only has the use of one of her arms. Her sight has diminished and her prognosis has not gotten better. She could be bitter. But she has decided to be appreciative for even the smallest things.

Although she has difficult days emotionally and physically, she fights every day to stay grateful and thankful.

She is still married, has a wonderful family and tons of friends who love her dearly. And she holds strong to her faith that God loves her.

Her life is not easy and her journey has many uncertainties, yet she's one of the most grateful people I know.

I truly believe the reason she has such a positive perspective on life is because she takes charge of her thoughts and focuses them in the right direction.

Although I don't know you, I know you have challenges in your life. But in the midst of them, there are still many things to be thankful for. Why don't you take a moment right now and list some of the things you are grateful for.

____

____

____

____

____

YOU NEED OTHER PEOPLE TO HELP YOU CHANGE YOUR THOUGHTS.

Relaunching and getting unstuck and beyond stress is not easy. More than likely you have been in your particular situation for a while. And I'm sure it's taken its toll on you.

Something I have discovered is that relaunching is much easier when you have people on the journey to help you. But the key to having people help you is that you have to ask. You can't be afraid or resist bringing people into your life to help you navigate the challenges.

Let's be honest. Most of us tend to be private people when it comes to our struggles and issues. Now you can't share your personal business with just anybody. You know that. But you need to share with somebody. Actually you need more than one person. One person alone cannot help you with everything you're going through. Don't try to do life on your own. You need people. You need relationships.

For example, if you're having challenges with your job, your spouse, your health, or any mixture of issues, you need various people with various knowledge, skills and experience to share wisdom with you in each particular area.

In fact, if you want to reach your goals in life, then part of your strategy should be reshaping your thoughts. That means you'll need individuals and support groups to help you accomplish that goal. Some of these people may already be in your life and some of them you'll have to seek out. In other words, you'll need to create your own customized support team.

Let's start with some of the qualities you need to look for in these individuals. Remember one person may possess a few of them, but you need to look for more than one person to serve different roles in your life. You need to find:

A person who will listen to your thoughts. This is an important person to find. This person will make the time to hear the ups and downs of what's going on in your life and they will be happy to help you. This person can handle your raw thoughts yet have the ability to help you find focus even in chaos. And after the conversation is over, you know everything you said will be held in confidence.

I know a lot of good people, but not all of those people are willing to make the time to listen to me. I say that because it may not be easy to find people who fit these roles, but don't give up. I know when I was ready to re-launch, I was like a detective looking for various people with the particular qualities I needed. Some I already knew and some were new relationships. Fortunately, I found them and I know you can, too.

A person who isn't afraid to be honest. Have you ever had something between your front teeth and discovered this yucky fact after talking to a room full of people? And people you know witnessed this embarrassing situation but no one told you? Well, have you ever been in that same situation but someone discreetly took you to the side and informed you of this embarrassing truth? Well, that's the kind of person you need in your life. Someone who isn't afraid to tell you the truth about your thoughts, even when they reveal something yucky about you.

A person who can find the humor in life. Sometimes we take ourselves too seriously. Sometimes our thoughts are so focused that we miss out on funny moments. Heck, sometimes you just need someone to laugh with. You probably know by now that everyone doesn't know how to have a good belly laugh. So when you find that friend who enjoys the funny moments of life, hang on to them.

A person who believes you're not crazy for dreaming big. Some people think it's absurd to start a business in this economy or leave one job for another. Sometimes when you share your big dream, whatever your dream is, you get that look. You know that look. That expression that says you've lost your ever-loving mind. Hopefully you have people in your life, or you are looking for people, who can support you in your big pursuits. If you don't have these people in your life, it's time to widen your circle. You need people who genuinely care about you and your dreams. These kinds of people will not only expect you to grow, they will become a part of the thinking process. When you find these people, they are worth holding on to.

YOU NEED A GOOD MENTOR TO HELP YOU WITH YOUR THOUGHTS.

As you look at the people you need in life, put a mentor on your list. Now a mentor may be the hardest person to find. But don't stop looking. When you find one, you'll see their value and understand.

After my business closed, I took a look at what contributed to my business failure. And one major factor was I didn't have a mentor. I didn't have someone to give me sage advice and teach me how to navigate the mess that sometimes comes along with not just business but with life in general.

A mentor will help you see that no matter how daunting your situation may seem, there's always room for possibility. They will also help you see the pros and cons of your situation. If nothing else, they will help stretch your thinking.

For example, a mentor will help you see that if you have to exit your job, it's wise to have a strategy—preferably a short-term strategy and a long-term one.

So how do you get a mentor? Look for them and ask them for help.

Be on the lookout for people living successful lives. You need to find someone whose life is being lived at some level of mastery or excellence and ask them to pour into you. If that person indicates that they don't have the time to spend with you on an ongoing basis, ask to take them to lunch. If they don't have time to go to lunch, do what I do. Steal mentoring moments.

Right on the spot ask if they have time for two questions. Most of the time a person will give you a couple of minutes and answer a couple of questions.

Of course, stealing mentoring moments isn't ideal if you really need to talk, but at least you have someone to help you out a little. Remember, your relaunch process will involve being creative with what you have.

So even if it's just a mentoring moment, seize it. That's what I had to do a lot of times.

RESHAPE YOUR THOUGHTS WITH GROWTH GROUPS.

Relaunching can be easier if you find a group of people who can help you. I discovered if you want to make a breakthrough, if you want to reach your goals, you have a greater chance of accomplishing them with the help of people who have similar interests. And people who are about getting results.

I must confess I wasn't always a proponent of groups. I was reluctant about opening up to people about my personal or professional life. Although I am an extrovert, I was a private person when I was going through the challenges on my job and in my depression. And I wanted to keep it that way.

Now I see being a part of a group as an advantage. You can benefit greatly from someone else's insights, thoughts, experience and wisdom.

There is a biblical proverb that says plans fail for lack of counsel, but with many advisers they succeed (Proverbs 15:22). The more help you get on your journey of transitioning out of stuck, the better you'll be.

If you need help, there is help. There are countless groups for everything you can imagine to help you along life's journey. Some are free and some are not. But it's comforting to know that you do not have to do life alone.

I'm a part of a couple of support groups. I like to call them growth groups because they are not a place to gripe and groan about the woes of life. These groups gather for one purpose. To help the individuals involved grow in the area they desire.

As a Christian, I have a group that helps me with my faith and spirituality. I have another group that helps me with my business and career. And I'm looking for one to help me with my health and wellbeing.

In each of these groups I have a network of people who gather together to exchange truth, insights, wisdom, knowledge, and experience.

Having been a part of these groups, I can tell you I wish I had incorporated this piece into my life sooner. As I look back on the wrong turns in my life, it was in part because I didn't allow other people to speak into my life. I didn't connect with enough of the right people to guide me.

In particular, I think about my past business experience. I had the passion for it but I didn't have enough knowledge to go along with it. I jumped into the playing field without knowing the rules. My hopes were high, but I bit off more than I could chew. I saw my business from the 50,000 feet level. I had the big picture crystallized, but my structure and systems were woefully inadequate. I was operating in areas where I had no expertise. And like many business owners, I was stretched too thin, going in too many directions, and making more decisions than I could handle. I was strained and doomed from the very beginning.

Please understand, I'm not saying my business would not have failed if I were a part of growth groups. But I do believe I would not have fallen as hard and as fast.

YOU CAN'T RELAUNCH AS HIGH AS POSSIBLE WITHOUT READING.

I know this question might sound stupid since you're reading this book, but do you like reading? If so, how often do you make time to read?

Okay, while you're wondering what that has to do with anything, let me share with you an experience I'll never forget.

Before my business closed, I was looking for financial help from anyone who was willing to help me. I tried everything I knew to try to save my hemorrhaging business.

Out of the blue, a friend who knew my business struggles called to say he knew of a guy who would probably be willing to give me some capital. Actually he was very confident this man would probably help me out because the man had given my friend some money for his business.

Now I wasn't sure what this person would want in return, but I was desperate to save my business. I probably would have given him up to half of the business just to keep it open. Remember I said I was desperate. Anyway, my friend set up the meeting.

On the day of the meeting, I dressed in my best business suit, I polished my business plan, and I wore a winning smile to match. Although I was nervous, I was confident. I was confident that I would be able to share with this investor that my business was worth his investment. But after about an hour of him asking me questions, I'll never forget what he said. He said, "I want to give you...." and at that moment my heart and mind began to race. I immediately began to think: Oh my goodness! How much is he going to give me? He then continued his sentence and said, "I want to give you some advice." What! Are you kidding me? Seriously?

You mean I did all of this preparing for some stupid advice. How in the world is your advice going to stop my business from financially bleeding to death?

Although I wanted to get up and leave, I graciously tried to fix my smile and act as if I was eager to hear his advice. He proceeded to tell me that I needed to read at least five various kinds of books. He said the first book I needed to read was a book on my philosophy of life. He said, "Since you're a Christian, you need to read the Bible." Ouch! I could tell he meant deeper than a casual read. And then he said I needed to read a book about business and a book for pure enjoyment. Hmmm. Maybe he should have added a book on how to deal with major disappointment. He went on to list two other kinds of books that I can't remember now. But his main point was that I needed to read.

If you're wondering if I took his advice the answer is yes and no. I did start reading my Bible more. But nothing else.

Shortly after my meeting with the investor, my business closed. And I still did not put his advice into practice.

Fast forward. I'm working at a job I hate. And every day I walked into the doors of that job, it felt like a noose was being tightened around my neck. It was at that point that the advice from the investor popped into my head: "You need to read."

Well, I thought, what did I have to lose? My life wasn't getting any better.

So I ventured onto the path of reading. Now I was still reading the Bible consistently. But I began to add business books, time-management books and all sorts of other books for my personal, professional and spiritual growth. And yes, I included in the mix a good book just for pure enjoyment.

I made time every day to read, even if it was listening to a book on CD.

Now catch this: I didn't have a lot of money so most of my books I bought from the thrift store. I was amazed at how many bestseller books I found on the shelves of many thrift stores. And on my lunch break I would visit the nearest bookstore and read the books I couldn't afford to purchase but needed the knowledge they contained.

I share that story with you because although at first I felt insulted by the investor's advice, it was some of the best advice I ever received. I can truly say my life has changed because of those books. The books I read have helped shape my thoughts in a positive way. I was empowered by their knowledge. And I felt more equipped to go to battle...whatever the battle was.

Now let's look at you and your story. You, too, need to be equipped and empowered for your personal battle.

So back to my original question. Do you read and how often?

Whatever your answer is, I hope my story encourages you to prioritize reading. I've discovered that great books help shape great thoughts.

So as we end this chapter, be encouraged. Yes, it will take mental conditioning to reshape your thoughts. But the payoff will be great. You'll be open to a whole new way of seeing life.

KEY# 3
USE THE RESOURCES YOU HAVE TO CREATE A RELAUNCH PLAN

The greatest accomplishment is not in never falling, but in rising again after you fall.

- Vince Lombardi

YOU HAVE TO START SOMEWHERE.
START WITH WHAT YOU HAVE.

"I don't have the support to pursue my dream."
"I can't afford to start a business."
"I want to write a book, but I don't know where to start."
"It's hard starting over again."
"I work so hard to have so little."
"I'm tired of struggling with...."

I'm not sure what's on your mind right now, but I'm sure a lot of thoughts are going on in your head. And that's the reason I have asked a ton of questions in this book. Questions are a great way to help you sort through your mountain of thoughts. And questions can be used as a tool to help you think deeper and wiser.

As you look at your life right now, you've probably wondered something like this. My life would be better if only I had:

- A better job.
- A supportive spouse.
- More money.
- More time.

We can all think of things we wish we had.

I'll be honest with you. You will never have everything you think you need at the moment you need it. There will always be a missing piece. The question is are you willing to use what you have to make a change in your life?

Right now you may have a micro-managing supervisor, a nagging spouse, disobedient kids, a broke-down car and jacked-up credit.

Whatever you're dealing with, I believe with everything in me, you can still relaunch right where you are.

Yes, you'll have to be creative, resourceful and unstoppable in your pursuit of reaching your goal. But you can do it. Yes, you may want to be somewhere else in life. But you're not. You are where you are. So position yourself right now to accomplish what you want later.

I discovered that most of the time I can accomplish what I want when I stop focusing on what I don't have. When I begin the process of looking for alternative ways to accomplish my goals, I always find them. As the old cliché says, there's more than one way to skin a cat. It's not a great cliché, but you get the point.

So in this chapter, let's turn our attention to the many ways you can use what you have right now to move forward. As you read, I want you to look at your skills, knowledge, experience, abilities, and people resources and see how you can use all of them to help you relaunch.

Some of the best resources you have are the ones you're overlooking. They're all around you. The question is, are you taking advantage of them?

WHERE YOU ARE CAN BECOME YOUR LAUNCHING POINT.

This is what I know about you. You want something to change in your life. That's the reason you're reading this book. You could be doing a ton of other things. Yet your desire is strong enough to seek out help. This is where

I come in. Because I realize, and you do too, that the change you want to see is going to take some time. How long? I don't know. But I do know you can speed up the change you want to see. How? Begin the launching process right where you are.

You may feel it's too difficult to do it right where you are. I understand. But if you can't leave your situation, you need to do something.

Don't just grind out another day in a slump and complain about it. Start stepping in the direction of your growth path. It's time to think strategically.

I wish we were sitting face-to-face because I would look you in the eye and tell you that whatever you're going through, whatever circumstances you find yourself in, this is the very place where you can launch. That's right. Your circumstances can be a springboard, a launch pad to your breakthrough. Think about that. What if you were on the brink of a breakthrough? What if you were mere days, weeks, or months away from experiencing life in a whole new way? Sometimes that's exactly how close we are to a change.

I am convinced that no matter where you are in life, you don't have to get stuck in it. You can become unstuck right where you are. And you can position yourself, no matter how uncomfortable it may be, to *relaunch*.

The question is: ***ARE YOU READY?***

SOMETIMES YOU JUST HAVE TO START OVER.

Here's the truth. Sometimes you just have to start over. No one really likes starting over. I know I don't. It feels like work just thinking about it. Well, that's because it is work. But it's rewarding work when you know that your efforts will position you to live life at a higher level.

Yes, you may have to start at the bottom. You may have to start in the last place you thought you would be. Maybe you're working at a job beneath your skills and expertise. Maybe you're a divorcee and it's hard to think about starting over after you've invested years in a marriage. Or perhaps you've been laid off from a job after you have purchased a home, two cars and sent children off to college. Perhaps you're starting life over on your own after losing someone you love. Maybe your health has deteriorated to the point that you have had to move in with someone. Or maybe you're having financial problems to the point that you have had to borrow money, when in the past you were the one others could come to for help.

Here's my point. Life for you right now may not be what you thought it was going to be. Yes, it's difficult to start over again or make a major transition. But is your life worth living at its optimum? Sure it is. And it's worth putting the time and effort into making the best of it. It's about seeing your life through new possibilities.

Yes, some things may have ended. But that only means something new needs to begin. So don't spend all your time focused on what used to be. Invest your energies on the new opportunities awaiting you.

THINGS HAVE CHANGED AND SO MUST YOU.

Sometimes you will have seasons in life where change is the last thing you want—especially if that means you might have to go it alone.

This story will illustrate my point.

Within a couple of years, I watched two friends' marriages end in divorce. Clearly divorce wasn't a part of their plans, but it happened. And I watched them both experience many emotionally tough days. At times both of them were so traumatized by the unfolding details of the divorce that they cried on my shoulder without restraint. The stages of grief began the moment they discovered that the divorce motions were in place. They also dealt with shock, disbelief, blame, and shame. Not to mention they both lost income, relationships, and a sense of security.

Although I haven't gone through a divorce, I know it's a terrible ordeal. If you're going through a divorce or have gone through one, my heart goes out to you. Many people have described it as a death. It's a terrible wound in a person's life.

For some people, it can take years to recover from the emotional, mental and psychological toll.

And one thing I've noticed about divorce is the power it has to keep a person stuck if they allow it to.

As I stood by both of my friends through their divorces, I noticed how different each person and situation was.

I noticed how over a period of time, one friend was able to begin the process of relaunching, while the other could not or would not allow herself to begin to start over.

Please understand, I know I'm not speaking from experience as a divorced woman, but I have experienced loss and pain. And I know that it's hard sometimes to bring yourself to the point of even seeing how a change can be beneficial.

But the key to any loss or setback is going through your pain and not setting up camp in it.

In some situations you need professional intervention or a support group to help you through it. That's what my one friend did who was able to relaunch. In her grief, she became proactive and sought out the necessary counseling she needed to help overcome her loss. While my other friend continued to keep her pain private. Only sharing with family and friends. She clung to her memory as a married woman. Her entire identity was wrapped up in what used to be. Whenever I would talk to her, she would manage to take the conversation back to the past. She would say things like, "I invested years in this marriage. How could he just walk away? What did I do to deserve this? How could he have done this to me?"

As you can tell, she was stuck on questions that she'll probably never get answers to.

The reality is divorce is hard. Any loss is hard. But you do have a choice in your pain. I love the way Ann Landers put it, *"Problems are inevitable. Misery is a choice."*

Now clearly I understand that two people will go through pain and, in this case, divorce differently. But if you want to relaunch from whatever your situation is, you have to do things differently than before.

I saw it clearly in the case of my friends. One friend saw divorce as the end of her life and the other saw it as a new beginning.

One friend looked at the pieces of a shattered marriage as all she had left. The other friend decided to take those same shattered pieces and start to build a great life.

When your old reality changes, it's time to begin the process of living with a new normal. If you're at a breaking point, allow it to be a catalyst to your breakthrough.

Relaunching is all about embracing change. Change that will move you closer to what you want on your growth path.

SOMETIMES STARTING FROM SCRATCH IS ALL YOU CAN DO.

My friends' stories illustrate that your life can change even without your permission. Fortunately, as long as you are alive you can take the broken and shattered pieces and make something great out of them. That's what relaunching and starting from scratch is all about.

Whatever your past situation may be, *there is an opportunity waiting for you to start over.* You've got to see life as a gift. The days, the weeks and the years are given to you to live, not to stay stuck.

You can relaunch. But you must decide that you want to. And that you are ready to do what it's going to take to relaunch.

That means if you need help, then seek it out. Don't try to do life on your own. If you need counseling or therapy, start your search today. Look for people who can help you take what you have and create a new beginning.

If you've been let go from a job, *then you get fired up*! Call your friends and family and let them know you're excited about your job search. Find out if they know of a company that needs your valuable skills. If you need more marketable skills, enroll in school or a certification program or call on a friend who has the expertise to teach you.

If it's a job or a relationship or whatever else you're seeking, know that you have something to offer. Present yourself with humility, but also with confidence. No one wants to hire or hang out with a victim. But there are plenty of people looking for people who are willing to contribute value wherever they go.

If you need to develop more skills in order to make yourself more valuable and marketable, start planning and doing what you need to do.

Don't be scared of starting at ground level in a company or in a relationship or wherever. *It's time to get excited about what you get to build from scratch.* Don't hang on to the old.

Listen, there are a multitude of options that are available to you if you begin to look at your life through the lens of possibilities. Don't focus on what you don't have. Focus on what you do have and make something of it.

NO TIME FOR EXCUSES. USE WHAT YOU HAVE AND DO SOMETHING DIFFERENT.

Let's not kid ourselves. Sometimes the hardest thing to do is to make yourself take action. It can be hard to relaunch. Many people will quit before they start. They quit by making excuses.

One thing I know for sure: If you want to start over again, you can. You can reinvent yourself. You can start from scratch. You can make the most of what you have. But you will have to get rid of your excuses.

Excuses will keep you tied down. And you know that. But we all make them.

The fact is no one has everything they need when they need it. You have to make the most of what you have.

Of course you'll find some people who seem to have it all. And don't worry about the fact that you don't have what someone else has. You have what you need right now—desire and a commitment to action. And the key is starting there and building momentum as you go along.

When I was a little girl my mom taught me, *"Use what you have and don't make excuses."*

When you think like this, you'll discover you have more available to you than what you could have ever imagined.

Before I wrote my first book, I had no idea what I was doing. I tried asking people for help, but no one I knew had any experience or expertise in writing a book. And when I did come across an individual with some experience, it didn't take long to figure out he was not going to mentor me in the process. And to his defense, he was a very busy man.

I remember asking him how to come up with a title? And he flippantly said, "Choose something pithy." Pithy? That's it. I need more help than that. But that's all the information he gave me and I used it. I added it to my arsenal of everything I needed to know about writing a book.

So the next thing I did was take my husband's advice. He told me to do what I knew how to do and be faithful at it and God would reveal more. So I knew the internet was full of information. I began to scour the internet for anything to help me learn how to write and publish a book.

I kept a file of what I was learning and I began to activate the process. And, by the way, I had no money. Or maybe I should say I had some money, but it was not even close to what it would cost to create a book on my own. But I was not going to allow that to stop me. I knew where there's a will, there's a way. And I had determined one thing. I had a choice. I could either moan about it or do something about it.

It took me a couple of years to write my first book because I didn't know what in the world I was doing. But I kept learning until I came up with a process that works for me. I even learned how to be my own independent publisher and how to contract out all the people I needed to bring my book to completion.

And thankfully, after two years, I had my first book in my hand.

Right about now you may be wondering where I got the money to print the books and hire the people. Well, being resourceful works. And so does a whole lot of praying!

I remember calling around for prices on everything I needed for my book. And I told everyone the story of my financial plight and how I really wanted to get my message out. Now I realized I had to pay something, but what I had was so little that it was next to nothing. I didn't whine and complain when I told my story. I just gave the facts, but with a positive attitude.

And I called people anyway. Some people I spoke with didn't care and I did understand. I know this is still business. Some listened to my story and said they couldn't help. But one lady listened and responded. She gave me a deeply discounted price on my book cover and interior layout. She even said I could pay her later when I started selling the books. She said she knew what it's like to start something new. She shared her story about how it was hard for her in the beginning of her business.

I was also able to get pre-orders on the book. And my story is history.

I share all of this because you will have to start with what you have.

If you want another job or different responsibilities in the company where you work, start looking at what you have to position yourself to get there. If you want to start a business, you will have to be creative with the resources you have. Who do you know that can help you? Where can you go to get help? How do you tell your story to people?

Keep looking for the best way to get what you want.

I remember when my speaking business began to grow and I came up with the idea of putting on my own conference. It was one of the scariest things I had attempted to do up to that point. In the beginning of my speaking business I played it really safe for the most part. Especially because of my history in my last business.

I decided to take a risk on the conference. But I thought it wise to take a very calculated risk. I had to live my dream, and that meant putting my money on the line for everything. The problem was I was working with a tight budget and very few people resources. But I was ready for a new level for my business and I needed to leave the bounds of safe living because there was just no excitement in it for me.

So let me share one resourceful thing I did on my tight budget.

I remember I listed all the things I needed on a piece of paper, and I thought there's no way I'd be able to get everything on my list within the time I needed it. But I remembered my mother's saying, "Use *what you have and don't make excuses.*"

So I began to break down my list item by item. I started with my need for signage. I needed signage for directions within the hotel and at the registration table and breakout rooms. So I went to a printing company and asked for a price. I nearly fell over when he quoted me the price. When he was finished, I asked if there were any other options—in particular, a lower option. He gave me another option. It still did not fit my budget. I then began offering suggestions of ways to cut costs. Can you believe that? I have no expertise in printing, but I do believe where there's a will, there's a way.

So after he gave me a very dismayed look, he thought for a moment and said, "I do have another option, but it won't be of the same quality." I asked if it would look professional and not cheap. He said, "Yes, it will look professional and it won't look cheap." I quickly responded, "Then that's the option I'll go with."

I got a great price. And I know one of the reasons is because I didn't give excuses. I used what I had. I exercised my creativity. And that's how I negotiated a lower price on everything on my list. And after the conference was over, I received rave reviews on how well done my conference was.

The point of this story is that many times you'll have to use what you have and do the best you can with what you have to reach your goals.

Now that we have talked about excuses, here are my questions.

- What excuses are you using?
- What progress are they preventing?
- And what resources (people resources, tangible resources) do you have to help you relaunch?

____

____

____

____

____

____

DO YOU KNOW WHAT YOU WANT IN LIFE?

As a professional speaker and author, I've traveled and met people all across this country. And I've talked to countless people about their life. Most people can tell me without even thinking what they don't like about their job, their marriage, or their relationship with their children.

But sadly, many of those same people cannot tell me what they really want in life, without hesitating and pausing for several minutes to think about it. Then again, I shouldn't be amazed. It wasn't until after my depression that I really began to realize what I wanted in life.

Sometimes it takes going through a valley or slump for us to realize that we need to start focusing on what we do want.

What do you want in life? What does your future look like to you? And how are you going to start planning your life from this point on?

I want you to think about that. Pray about it. Dream about it. Wrestle with it.

To help you sort out your thoughts, I'm going to give you some space to write about your future. Take some time to dream on this paper. Think on this paper. Cry on this paper if you have to, but write what's deep in your heart. Write the things that may scare you to death. Write the things that you have always felt too inadequate for or unworthy of doing. Write those things down that you're not sure of, but you wish and hope will come true.

This is your time to dream, plan and envision.

As you think about your future, break it down into small daily steps. How do you want your future to start shaping up in the next month? Six months? Or year? Don't be afraid to put a timeline on your plan. You may have to change the date, but challenge yourself to have one.

DO YOU KNOW WHAT YOUR PASSIONS ARE?

Do you know what fires you up?

Relaunching and getting past stuck and stress is also about connecting to what frees you up to enjoy life. Those activities that cause you to lose track of time whenever you do them.

As I shared with you earlier, I've talked with a lot of people in my lifetime. Sadly, not only do many people not know what they want for their future. Many are not even aware of their passions.

Many people don't know what they love to do. Or if they do know, many people say they're too busy to do it.

Come on. I know you're under stress and pressure, but you still need to do things that get you pumped up. A surefire way to go into a slump is to not make time to engage in your passions.

The reality is life is too hard and too short not to enjoy it.

As you can tell, I am big on people living out their passions and loving what they do. But I also know the reality is you may not be able to participate in your passions with the current job you have. However, be as creative as you can to use the time and resources you have to do things you enjoy.

If your situation at work is challenging, then you need some excitement from the outside to overflow into your job.

I recently shared a "passion" principle with someone I was coaching. This client was dealing with boredom and monotonous work on her job. Fortunately this person was about to go on a cruise. And as you would suspect, she was extremely excited. This gave me a great segue into my next question. I asked her, "Does your excitement about the upcoming cruise stop when you get to work?" She replied, "No." I then shared with her this key piece of advice. Continue to do things that will ignite your heart so that it overflows into your job. That's the passion principle. When you're passionate, it overflows into everything you do. Even though there are other issues with the job, the key is to navigate your situation so you can experience happiness at work. Even if that happiness is flowing from the outside.

My brothers are crazy busy at work. And their tendency, like many of us, is to put themselves on the back burner. But they share a passion. Fishing. So they have become accountability partners for each other, reminding each other to take a passion break and go fishing.

Now that's not a passion of mine and never will be. But it doesn't matter. They love it and that's what counts.

I do have several passions. Believe it or not, I now love to read books. I can get swept away in a good book. I love to speak and help people move forward in their life. I love to sing to God and about God. I love to take cruises and vacations with my family. And I love to shop garage sales and thrift stores. I love to find treasures at these places.

Yes, I know someone is reading this and thinking, "What? You like to do that?" Yes, I do. It gets me excited to find a $100 item for three bucks.

Well anyway, back to you. What do you love to do? If you don't know your passions, explore them with these questions:

- What makes you giddy like a little child when you're doing it?
- What activity makes you lose track of time?

- What could you talk about for hours if given the opportunity?
- What do you like to do that benefits other people?

I ask you these questions because your answers to them are a sign of what you're passionate about. You not only need to know what they are, but you need to do them.

This is what I want you to do. Make a list of your passions and then write down how you will incorporate them into your schedule.

____

____

____

____

____

DO YOU WANT A JOB OR BUSINESS THAT ALLOWS YOUR PASSION TO BE RELEASED?

I know there's no perfect job or life, but why not try to find the best fit for your career, business or situation that allows your passions to flow. I know some people believe only a few people ever live out our passions in our job. Whether that's true or not, I want to be one that does. How about you?

Here's my perspective. I have been given only one life, not two or three. So the question I wrestle with is what will I do with my one life? What will you do with yours?

I'm focusing a lot on passion because it's one of the best ways to use what's inside of you to get past stuck and stress and begin your relaunch.

Let me share my passion story.

Over a decade ago I played a role in helping bring an international speaker to the city where I lived. Although I played a small role in comparison to the organizer, this speaker said she wanted to meet me in person to say thank you. So on the day of the conference, when my presence was requested, I left my front-row seat and went behind the curtains. I strolled back into a hallway hidden away from the crowd of thousands. Imagine how special I felt to meet this renowned Christian speaker.

After we greeted each other with a hug and exchanged a few words, I will never forget her prayer. As we held hands, I silently prayed a very spiritual prayer: *God, please don't let my hands start sweating.* With that thought on my mind, I listened intently to her prayer. Maybe you shouldn't be impressed with a prayer, but how many times would I get to hear this woman, who knows Greek better than anyone I know on the earth, pray a prayer over me.

I was immediately amazed. She didn't pray like a Greek scholar. She didn't pray like a halo was on her head. She just prayed a child-like prayer. No pretenses. No righteous-sounding words. Just simple, everyday words on my behalf to God.

She uttered a simple sentence, "Father, I pray that the deepest dream of Kim's heart will come true." Of course she said other words, but I was stuck on that one sentence.

That one sentence in her prayer involved the passion of my heart. After she finished, I gave her a quick hug and glided back to my seat. I felt like I was walking on clouds. Her prayer ignited once again the fire in my heart and my passion to write a book. And also my dream of being a national speaker. I realized that day that I had allowed many things to distract me from the passion of my heart.

I also realized that it was going to be a struggle to see that passion become reality because of the obstacles I faced. But I knew if I nurtured my passion and did something daily to help my passion grow, eventually my dream would become a reality.

The first thing I had to do was fight my self-doubt we talked about earlier. And I had to fight my negative thoughts and look at the possibilities beyond my current situation.

You see, I was flat broke. I'm talking about the kind of broke where pennies matter and dollars are like gold. And my second problem was that I had never really written anything in my life.

So here I was holding a dream in my heart and I lacked the necessary writing skills and the money needed to make the dream come true. Not to mention, I had no friends in high places to help make it happen.

And then I remembered the worst part of all. I felt like a prisoner to my job.

But that day I took action. I made a short-term and long-term exit plan on how I was going to transition out of my job. But while I was doing that, I grew my passion for the dream I believed God had given me. Now I knew

I couldn't control outside variables, but I could control and take charge of my part.

I began to write every day. Even when I didn't know what I was doing, I wrote. Eventually I began to search the internet for help. And when my finances improved, I began to go to writers' conferences. I was determined not to allow my passion to dwindle.

Living out my passion persistently allowed me to relaunch and live out my dreams. And I can say, dreams do come true— even for broke people— if you grow your passion.

Below are two factors that helped me to feed my passion.

I became a consummate learner. I became a student. I devoured any book I could get my hands on. Books on writing, on starting a speaking business, and on expanding my career. As I've nurtured my passion with knowledge, I've grown in competence as well as confidence. Knowledge will help open your mind to new information and help open doors for you, too. If you continue to learn and embrace what you're learning, you won't stay stuck.

I used my commute as my classroom. You can grow your passion on the go. On your commute to work, make your car a mobile university. Or if you commute by a transit system, listen on your phone or tablet to the countless free downloads of content that experts are giving away. Once I discovered this strategy, it fueled my passion on my way to work and on my way home. I then extended it to my home life by injecting it into my daily schedule. When I was washing dishes, ironing clothes or repairing something in the house, I made my home a library of learning. I listened online to experts give an abundance of insights, knowledge, tips and tools on anything I need to know. Believe me, you don't have enough time in your life to take in all the free information that's on the internet.

As you begin to do this, watch how your passion is fueled for your dream and for the things you want. Watch how your passion will even overflow into every area of your life.

ARE YOU AIMING HIGH ENOUGH?

Do you sense that there is so much more you can do with your life? I hope you do. Just think about this: What chapters have yet to be written about your life?

Earlier, when I asked you to write down your vision of your future, how did you feel? Did you stretch yourself in your thinking, in your desires and ambitions? Or did you settle for less than the best for your life in any area?

I'm asking you that question because sometimes we don't aim as high as we could. If we're honest, sometimes we limit our goals and dreams just in case we don't achieve it. It's a way of protecting ourselves. Sometimes we aim lower than what we know we can achieve because it insulates us from disappointment.

Think about it. No one plans on being mediocre. Yet far too many people are just mediocre in terms of how they live life. How does that happen? Somewhere along the way they settled into comfortable, safe living.

Let me ask you this:

- What limits have you placed on yourself?
- Do you feel you are capable of more?
- Describe what you think you can do more of or be better at.

What do you feel compelled to do in the next year? 5 years? Before you die?

Describe how you will feel once you accomplish some of your goals?

____

____

____

____

____

To aim high you will have to stretch your thinking. You will have to see larger possibilities for your life and begin to act on what you see.

Stop waiting around for things to be just right. Begin to plan and then take action using what you have. Now I'm not asking you to do anything rash. Rather, I'm hoping you won't delay in putting your goals and desires into motion. Planning says you are serious about what you want. And action says you're not going to settle for a mediocre life.

DON'T ALLOW THE DISTRACTIONS TO AFFECT YOUR GROWTH.

Once you have your future in sight, you'll have to become keenly aware of anything or anyone who has the potential to distract you from growth. If you're going to stay on course, you'll need to be aware of the things that have the power to derail you on your journey.

Look at the activities in your day. Make a list of anything that can be distracting. For example, how much time do you spend watching television, participating in social media (Instagram, Twitter, Facebook, Pinterest), or on any other activity outside of your job.

Ask yourself these questions:

- What activities am I allowing to rob me of time that I need to work on my relaunch?
- What can I do to remind myself to stay focused?

____

____

____

____

____

____

It's impossible to make a relaunch if you are weighed down with nonessentials. So what are the essential activities you need to activate in your life and what are the nonessentials you need to de-activate or decrease?

Here is my suggestion: Break down your day.

Ask yourself these questions:

- What should I do every day that will increase my chances of a successful relaunch?
- What could I begin to do for at least five minutes a day that would have a compound effect, yield results, and help me improve my life?

Take some time to write out your thoughts.

____

____

____

____

____

You may be thinking... five minutes? What can I do with five minutes? Well, you can get a lot done over time with five minutes. If you use this five-minute rule, it will help you get started on your plan and remove your excuses. Who doesn't have five minutes out of twenty-four hours? It's hard to make an excuse when you only need five minutes of time to make something happen.

If you commit to five minutes every day, chances are you'll end up putting in even more time. But at the minimum, you'll know you're making five minutes' worth of progress. In five minutes you can make a phone call that you have been putting off. You can write an email and send it off. You can send someone your resume. If you don't have a resume, you can begin researching and writing one with your five minutes. You can begin reading a book with your five minutes. You can set up a networking meeting with a friend.

You get the picture. So what are you going to do with your five minutes?

A few years ago, I had the privilege of spending time with the owner of Dunbar Armored. He was kind and personable. It didn't take me long to be impressed with this man. Not only because of his accomplishments, but because he took time to pour into me. He asked questions about my life. He wanted to know my story and how I began my career as a speaker.

Before I left, Mr. Dunbar gave me some sage advice that I will never forget. He said, "Kim, I always tell my children that robberies never just happen. They're always planned." I took away from his message that I needed to plan my success and also to be aware of anything that had the potential of robbing me of it.

The one thing I remember clearly about my old job is the desperation I had for something to change quickly. And because I knew it would probably be a while before I could quit, I put a 30-day plan in place that I repeated month after month until I made my exit.

You see, I have a little bit of Attention Deficit Disorder. I have a hard time focusing. So I needed to plan everything in bite-size pieces for short periods of time. It works. I have written six books using this method. I need short-term planning that I can do over and over again that will yield lasting results.

The key is to know yourself and what works best for you. If you want to do something different, go right ahead. Here's my 30-day plan. It's a simple but powerful one.

Create milestones for your future.

Once you have a vision for your future in your head and you begin to plan it out, you will need help to stay on target. Milestones are the markers to help you evaluate and assess your progress. Milestones become the tangible parts you can see that help you know whether or not you're reaching your goals. As you think about milestones, what will yours be?

One of the best ways to begin creating your milestones is to write them down.

Write out your plan.

I know some people reading this are thinking: I don't want to take the time to write out my plan. I can keep it in my head. I know what I want to do.

Yes, you can keep your plan in your head. But research has proven that when you write your goals down, you have a greater chance of achieving them. This may shock you, but I don't like to write out plans. The reason I do it is because I know the value and benefit of doing it. And I learned a long time ago not to let my feelings block my progress.

If you start now with a plan, how much progress do you think you can make in the next 30 days? Make a realistic blueprint of how you can improve your life. Don't make it hard. Just activate your five-minute strategy.

Have a specific time of the day
to activate your plan.

If you want to see your plan realized sooner, become consistent in working on it at a particular time of day when distractions won't crowd it out. Then when you get

into a rhythm and routine of doing something productive and progressive, it will feel strange *not* to do it.

Benefits of Having a Plan

- You will gain clarity of mind and heart
- You will separate yourself from the average person
- You will be inspired to make your desires happen
- You can track your progress
- You'll be able to break out of your old routines and habits that are no longer benefiting you
- You'll know where to spend your time and attention

Now get fired up! Put a deadline on your plan.

The best way to move your life towards the future you want is to know what you want and why you want it. Then add a deadline to your plan and it will have you emotionally charged up. You will be like a locomotive charging down the tracks every day. Ralph Waldo Emerson wrote, "The world makes way for the man who knows where he is going."

When you add action to a plan, it's as if you put feet on it and it's always in motion, moving you closer to your desired future.

Ask yourself a question that will keep the momentum going.

Ask yourself: *What is the wisest thing I should do today?* The more you do this, the more you'll realize that there are countless options, possibilities, and avenues where you can choose to get unstuck and get on your way to relaunching.

Now put your plan in a place where you can visually see it every day.

Visuals are powerful. But they're just tools. There's no magic in visuals. The visual is simply there to remind you it's time to put some work into what you say you want. Visuals say: Make wise choices now! The clock is ticking. Don't put off what you say you want.

Tell at least one person about your plan.

If you ask someone you trust to hold you accountable to your action plan, you are more likely to follow through. Because you have a greater chance of following through when you know someone is going to ask you about your progress.

To keep me on track with writing my first book, I told several people about it. I also called them on a regular basis to give them an update on my progress. Turns out they were more excited than I thought. I discovered on my down days (and I did have down days) they were some of my biggest cheerleaders. I'm so glad I did not do that journey on my own. Since it turned out to be so beneficial for me, I have continued this process with each book and on all of my goals.

So who are you going to tell about your plan?

BECOME DECISIVE.

Whatever you do, don't be passive about it. Stop stalling. Take your life off of pause. Yes, you need to take precautions. But being cautious does not mean being passive. If you embrace passivity, you are going to stay stuck longer than you want to.

As you become more in tune to the future you want, you must become more deliberate. You must become a person of action. In your decisions, calculate the pros and cons, but make a move. Sometimes we can be so worried about making a mistake, that we become paralyzed in inaction. Don't be afraid to go where you have never been. Yes, you may fumble forward, but at least you are moving and you can adjust along the way.

AVOID THE TRAP OF PROCRASTINATION.

Progress or procrastination… it's your choice.

My friend, you are loaded with potential. Everyone is. But the majority of people do very little with their potential. Why? We allow procrastination to rule our lives.

Are you doing that?

If you're like most of the world, you struggle with procrastination—putting things off, delaying things, waiting until tomorrow to do something you could do today. The problem with that approach is tomorrow is loaded down with undone tasks from last week and last month.

When you procrastinate you are working against yourself. Procrastination is the enemy of progress. When you put something off that needs to be done today, you slow down success.

In order to make sure you don't get stuck, you'll have to fight your own resistance to making the necessary changes. Procrastination can be one of the greatest enemies to any plan, but especially to relaunching

In many cases, most of us know what to do, but we put it off.

For example, if you are looking for a job, you can't afford to procrastinate. You can't embrace the *I'll do it tomorrow syndrome.* You must seize the opportunities at hand. How? By becoming active every day in doing something, no matter how small. Do something every day to reach your goal.

Here's a personal story to illustrate my point.

Our son graduated from college and, from a statistical point of view, most college students don't get into the field of their choice or make the money they thought they were going to make right after college.

So the day after our son received his college degree, he came back home to live with us. He had no job. No money. And no car. Instead of procrastinating and allowing himself to become discouraged, he chose to become active in his job search. As a part of his strategy, he became diligent in doing the things he knew would help bring about the job he desired. He sent out resumes. He searched online job sites. He informed family and friends that he was looking for a job. He made phone calls. He interviewed. He networked. And he received a lot of nos. But he kept trying.

Now I'm an early riser, but he would beat me getting up in the morning. He made it his job to look for a job. When he finally discovered a position that matched his skills and passions, he went after it. And so did 200 other people. Wow! Two hundred people applied for one position. Yes. But don't run past this: There was one job and it was available for one person. And he believed he was that one person. And he got that job!

Ultimately, he persevered. He took his big vision, aimed high, broke down his goals into manageable parts, and every day took intentional action steps toward it. He made his relaunch from unemployment to being employed.

My question for you is: Why can't *you* be that *one* in whatever situation you're hoping for?

You can be the one to reach your dreams. You can be the one to relaunch. You can be the one to make the most of what you have. And you can be the one who doesn't procrastinate yourself out of your dreams.

WHEN YOU THINK YOU HAVE TRIED EVERYTHING . . .

Ask Yourself: So...What Else?

When I was going through my life coach certification several years ago, I learned a powerful phrase. In class we had to watch a powerful video of a master life coach in a session with a client. This particular client wanted to be a speaker and she felt stuck with what to do next. She was so frustrated because she felt like she had exhausted all of her options of trying to break into the speaking business.

Now this video really piqued my interest since I'm a professional speaker. As I watched the video I wanted to jump into the screen and shout: *Keep trying. You haven't exhausted all your options.* Because I'm a speaker, I knew there were more ways to break into the business than what she listed.

After the coach listened to her explain everything she had tried, he looked intently into her eyes and with a calm assuring voice asked her this question, "What else?"

She immediately fired back, "I've tried everything."

He again posed the question, "What else?"

As he waited in silence for a response, she realized he wasn't going to let this go. She thought for a moment, and then she began slowly coming up with an idea she had not thought about. Again, the coach asked, "What else?" This process went on for several minutes until he realized she had exhausted her capacity to come up with ideas. When she finished, he offered some suggestions of his own.

Do you see the point in this story?

There is more available to you than you realize. When you think you're out of options—when you think you're stuck—just pose this question to yourself, "What else?"

KEY# 4
PREPARE FOR CRITICAL CONVERSATIONS TO JUMP-START YOUR JOURNEY

"The one thing you can't take away from me is the way I choose to respond to what you do to me. The last of one's freedoms is to choose one's attitude in any given circumstance."

- Holocaust survivor Viktor E. Frankl

SPEAK UP BUT DON'T GET STUCK.

In the previous chapters I had you doing some internal and introspective work. In the next two chapters, we will look at how to successfully interact with people so you don't get distracted from your growth path. I'm sure you already know that whenever you have to deal with people, there is work involved. And in this chapter the work involves having critical conversations or strategic confrontations with certain people. More than likely you've been putting off a conversation you need to have with someone. Hopefully what you learn in this chapter will help you move forward and have that conversation.

So how do you speak up when you need to and not get stuck?

Here are some important strategies to help you.

INVEST YOUR TIME AND ENERGY IN THE RIGHT SITUATION.

You're probably facing a lot of challenging issues in your life right now. If that's the case, you'll more than likely need to have critical conversations with certain people. However, only you can decide if a situation or person warrants your time and energy.

Let me share this story and then I'll explain.

Some time ago I was under a lot of pressure with my business. I was facing deadlines on some important projects. My stress was high and my patience was low. And on this one particular day I needed to go pick up some needed items from the department store. I knew that the closest store to me was one of the busiest. But I was hoping not to run into a crowd. But sure enough I did. The parking lot was packed. So like most wonderful drivers, I drove around looking for that coveted parking spot near the door.

After driving around for far too long, I decided I would have to park miles from the store. Well, not really. It just seemed like it.

I finished my shopping and headed back to my car. As I was approaching my car, I quickly decided to push the cart off to the side so I didn't have to walk the cart back. But as I was getting into my car, someone angrily barked out to me, *"Put that cart back!"*

I quickly turned around to see who it was. Was it a manager? An overzealous employee?

No. It was a middle-aged lady who had apparently deputized herself as the unofficial shopping cart police. I'm wondering what you're thinking right about now. And what you would have done.

I guess I better give you some quick background information before I continue. My teenage daughters were with me and I had been teaching them the importance of owning their attitude. I had shared with them the importance of not giving anyone the power to change your disposition or distract you from your goals. I didn't expect I would have to put my advice into practice in a parking lot.

Regardless, even with only a couple of seconds to gather my thoughts, I knew I had to make a choice. I could fire back at this mean-spirited lady and scold her for yelling at me. Or I could get on with my life and go back home and work on my important projects.

In case you're wondering, I was boiling inside. But again, I have a responsibility to control me. I had to make up my mind in a split second because believe me this lady was prepared to engage in a war of words. A heated debate was not on my agenda, so I decided I was going to be in control of my emotions. I was not going to let her or anyone else hijack my day. Furthermore, I had decided months earlier I was only going to invest my time and energy in the right situations. I was no longer going to give my precious time and energy to just anybody.

Even though this situation was unexpected, I had been preparing myself to keep my mind focused and my life moving forward. And because of that, I knew this lady was a potential distraction and I was not going to allow her to take me off course and get me stuck in a stupid argument.

And it turned out there was a place to put the shopping cart not too far from my car. So I took it and rolled it into the space. I didn't say a word to the lady. But my silence spoke volumes. She was beyond shocked. She looked confused and deflated. This was not what she expected. She wanted some type of verbal engagement. She thought she was going to have the spotlight in my life, at least for a few moments. But she wasn't getting it from me.

The truth is, I was more powerful without words. And I enjoyed every step I took back to my car. I knew I was stepping up my game. And that I owned my attitude.

Maybe you would have responded differently in this situation. But everyone that ticks you off doesn't deserve your time or energy. On the other hand, there are times when you shouldn't walk away. Some situations are worth confronting. Just make sure they're ones that will help you move forward or grow in some way.

This chapter is about helping you with those critical conversations you need to have with people. And, as uncomfortable as it may be, embracing the value of communicating effectively is a must on your growth path and in helping you relaunch.

SOME SITUATIONS ARE WORTH TAKING ACTION.

Last year I met a professional lady in the community. She seemed to have it all together on the outside, but this lady had more than her share of challenges on her job. We talked for over an hour, and in that time I discovered how frustrated and disappointed she was. She couldn't believe the ugly facts she was beginning to learn about the company she worked for. When she took the job, she had great expectations. She thought it was going to be a place where she could use her knowledge and skills to help the company grow and a great place to advance in her career. But the opposite was true.

She shared with me times when senior management took credit for her work, and the many times she was overlooked in meetings. She continued to share how she didn't feel challenged by the job responsibilities. And she was coming to the realization that the culture of this company had been this way long before she came on the scene.

As she continued to talk, I realized she was emotionally venting about her situation. And she needed to.

However, there comes a time when a person has to move from venting to determining their next strategic moves.

I'm sure you may be thinking, why didn't she just quit?

Well, like many people, she couldn't quit. She couldn't afford to. I'm sure many times she wanted to run into her boss's office with her resignation papers in hand. I'm sure she wanted to take her knowledge and skills somewhere else. But for now, she had to stick it out. She needed to stay. And like many people, she felt stuck.

The reality is whether she stayed or prepared to leave, she needed to see this situation as a growth opportunity. She could either seize it and grow or she could shrink back and continue to be stuck. This was her chance to leverage her frustration to help her grow.

This was an opportunity for her to regroup and discover how to navigate her unique situation. She needed to see how she could make the best of a bad situation. It was time to look at all viable options.

So I started with some simple questions. I asked her if she had tried talking to anyone about her concerns. I continued by asking her if there were any ways she could create more challenging opportunities for herself inside and outside her job.

After asking a few questions, she looked stunned. Probably because she had spent so much time focusing on what she couldn't do that she hadn't been looking for solutions within her limitations and restrictions.

I spent the next hour or so helping her chart out her next move. I wanted her to think hard about any ways she could position herself within that job so that she could have some sense of fulfillment.

I certainly knew it would be difficult to walk through the doors of that job on most days, but if she became intentional about growing personally and professionally within her limitations she would be positioning herself for more opportunity. Whenever you make the decision to progress within your limitations, you are positioning yourself to experience life at a level most people will never see.

I wanted her to see that sometimes your life will look more like a maze than an open map with clear direction. Sometimes it will be difficult to get where you want to go. But if you continue searching, looking, and persisting, you'll find a way to navigate through your maze and find the opening you are looking for.

I understood this job situation wasn't going to be easy for her. Why? Because most of us put more focus on the problems than we do finding workable solutions. Now it may not be perfect solutions, but it can work to help decrease the stress. As she began to think about her next strategic moves, she realized:

She needed to have a conversation with key players in her senior management to express her concerns.

She needed to become more assertive and proactive within meetings and not take the victim stance.

She needed to use better judgment as to who she shared information with on the job.

She also recognized that she displayed more of a defensive posture than she should.

Her attitude on the job revealed she wasn't happy. And as we talked, she embraced the reality that bad attitudes are not the solution. If anything, bad attitudes will back-fire on you.

She had never really thought about her situation as a *growth opportunity*. But this was her opportunity to grow personally and professionally right where she was. This was an opportunity to grow her competence, her character, and her skills in navigating the company culture.

After we finished talking, I knew that although she was armed with tools and tips, this would still be a process. But now she was fueled and ready to start the process and begin her great relaunch.

AVOIDING NEEDED CONVERSATIONS CAN PUSH BACK YOUR RELAUNCH.

Right now you can probably think of at least one person you need to have a critical conversation with.

Honestly, most of our challenges are with people. The reality is that the closer two or more people work together or live together, the greater the chance to offend, misunderstand, and irritate one another. No matter how wonderful a person is, at some point you may feel offended, devalued, or taken for granted.

The complexity of relationships will never go away. Someone will inevitably get under your skin. Someone will rub you the wrong way. Someone will test your last nerve.

And the issue may be with a boss or co-worker, with a spouse or significant other, or with a child or family member. Whoever it is, you shouldn't avoid having candid conversation. Because unsettled issues can keep you bogged down and make it hard for you to relaunch.

So have you been putting off having a critical conversation with someone?

Most people do.

Some people admit to not having needed conversations because of past experiences when things didn't go well.

Some say they know that if they share their feelings, the other person may have a hard time handling what they have to say.

And some people shared with me that they have tried communicating about an issue with a particular person and felt the conversation didn't produce the results they hoped for. So they try to avoid any type of confrontation.

And some have admitted that they have just given up trying.

Please hear me. Avoiding confrontation and that needed conversation is not the answer. So how do you position yourself to have that needed talk?

LAY THE GROUNDWORK BEFORE HAVING A CRITICAL CONVERSATION.

There's one thing that's certain in life besides death and taxes. That is, you can't avoid conflict in relationships.

So the best defense is an offense. Be prepared.

No one wants drama. But if drama comes knocking on your door, open it and be ready for the situation.

Disagreements will happen. You already know that. You've had your share in your life. Some you will never forget. And in some, you wish you could have a do-over.

Critical conversations are never comfortable. Many times we go in knowing what will likely happen. Hurt feelings and misunderstandings. While that may not be your intention, it sometimes does happen. But the goal of the conversation should always be finding solutions to keep things progressing and moving forward.

In relaunching your life, you can't avoid having these needed conversations, so be prepared to engage people in the most effective way.

Have a conversation with yourself. Okay, the first part of the communication plan is to get yourself ready. Before having a confrontation with someone, you need to be as emotionally prepared as possible. I know it can be awkward and uncomfortable to confront anyone. I won't pretend that it's easy. I actually dread the process, but I love the outcome—I GROW!

You may need to have a personal pep talk to remind yourself to stay calm and to stay on the issue at hand.

Sometimes just getting ready to talk to someone about an issue can get your blood boiling when you imagine various scenarios. And if you are like most people, we're good at imagining the worst possible outcome.

Here's the reality. You can't control how a person will respond. You will always have that uncertainty. But you can prepare yourself for the conversation. You can determine the words you will and will not use. You can be emotionally under control rather than being emotionally charged.

The key is to not lose sight of how important it is to have this needed conversation so you can keep moving forward in life. Don't give up on doing the work it's going to take to make progress. So if that means having a conversation to hash out facts and feelings with someone, you can do it in the best way possible.

Remember, you need to become a better communicator. Not just to master words, but to master your emotions while communicating.

Vent forward with someone before the conversation. Everyone needs a sounding board. Do you have one? If not, find someone you trust who will listen to your raw emotions and give you wise counsel when you are finished venting. Everyone needs a person in their life who can help them keep their focus in the middle of a mess. Just make sure you allow this person the freedom to give you candid feedback. Sugar coating doesn't help you grow.

I thank God for my husband and for my best friend, two people I talk to when I'm mad about an issue. Since I deal with so many people in my line of work, I have to have many uncomfortable conversations. But before I do, I talk to my husband and my friend so they can help me stay on track. Unfortunately they have to hear a lot of my raw emotions. And thankfully, they help me filter and sift through the thoughts I should share and the ones I should keep to myself. They remind me of the importance of word choice, tone and timing. So at the end of the day, they help me to vent forward.

Understand how you communicate. Knowing yourself is important. The more self-aware you are, the better prepared you can be for your crucial conversation. You should not be a stranger to yourself. You should know what kind of personality you have. You should know your trigger points and pain points. You should be able to identify when your tone of voice is not what it should be. You should be aware when a non-verbal is contradicting the message coming out of your mouth.

With that thought in mind, reflect back to as many times as you can when you have had to have crucial conversations. What was your behavior like? What are your tendencies? Be as honest as you can be.

Having spoken with many people that I know well, I've learned that some of them don't have an accurate assessment of themselves. Like many people, they see themselves in the most positive light.

The truth is we all have strengths and weaknesses and we need to know them. And one of the best ways to get a better picture of yourself is to ask people you trust how they view you in terms of strengths and weaknesses. Or if you prefer, ask them about any areas where you could use improvement.

In the professional world some companies provide a 360-degree review for their employees. They gather information from people who interact with each person in all areas of their life.

If you do a 360-degree review, you may be surprised at people's responses.

A few years ago I had an informal and unexpected review with my family. I must admit, I didn't see some of the gaps where I needed to grow until they spelled it out for me. Honestly, I wanted to refute their comments, but we were having a great time just sitting around talking. So I knew it was not coming from a place of malice.

Although it was hard to hear, I needed that truth so I could grow and develop. That day I got a dose of my own advice. I had to put developing my communication skills on my growth path.

Read up on communication strategies. After our conversation, I began to scour the internet for help. I also read books and articles on how I could become better at communicating. I have improved, but I still have a ways to go.

Here's the thing. No one is born a great communicator. So if you want to be confident in getting your message across, you need to find resources to help you communicate better.

It is my hope that this chapter will encourage you to invest in becoming the best communicator you can be. While there are no simple answers, being a good communicator can make a difference in making inroads and it can have tremendous impact in your situation and in all of your relationships. Your relaunch is connected to your communicating better.

As you think about communication, let me ask you some questions.

Where do you need to improve in your communication?

____

____

____

____

____

____

What steps are you going to take to improve?

____

____

____

____

____

____

TIME TO HAVE THE CRITICAL CONVERSATION.

Most of us are skilled at using words. But how skilled are we at using the right words when we are upset? Words, in and of themselves, are not the issue. It's how we use them when talking with other human beings who have emotions, feelings, and memories. We've all been guilty of allowing the conversation to become a war of words.

So how can we guard ourselves against this?

Establish boundaries before the conversation. It's easier to have conversations when boundaries are clearly established. Before bringing up a topic of discussion, make sure you have healthy boundaries set up for yourself. And if at all possible, share with the person you are about to have a conversation with that your intentions are to talk and listen to resolve an issue. You can also display your boundary lines by refraining from raising your voice, interrupting, or saying anything that would be considered below the belt. Try not to insert the words "never" or "always" into the conversation. That is a quick way to take the conversation off course. These are just a few things to remember as you converse. The point is to have a line that you will not cross and to hold yourself to that boundary.

Take a deep breath. Don't take breathing for granted. You not only need it to live, but taking a deep breath is a calming mechanism. Studies have proven that when you take a deep breath, you lower your cortisol levels which reduces your stress and anxiety.

Have a list of conversation starters.

I'm sure you probably have conversation starters of your own. But I thought I would share a few ideas on how to initiate a critical conversation.

- "Can I speak to you about a concern of mine?"
- "I'm wondering are you sensing any tension, because I am?"
- "Can you help me understand what happened in that meeting?"
- "There are a few things that are bothering me. Can we talk?"
- "I need to talk to you, what is a good time for us to speak?"

Don't overload the conversation. Most people stuff their emotions until they can't take it anymore. Then by the time they're ready to talk, they bombard the individual. While it's tempting to solve as many issues as you can in one conversation, try not to. Pick your battle. Don't try to win the war when you enter into a critical conversation. People can only handle so much at a time.

Let me give you some advice that I learned the hard way. As difficult as it may be:

- Be as specific as possible.
- Share facts, not just feelings.
- Avoid pettiness. Prioritize what is most important.

Remember, people can only digest so much before they vomit up vengeance.

Remember to own your attitude. Always be calm and in control. Now believe me, I know there are some people that can push our buttons if we allow them to. So you must make up your mind that you will have control of yourself. Have you ever said that someone made you mad? Well I heard someone respond to that comment by saying, "Mad was already in you. That person just knew how to bring it out." So before having that difficult conversation, check your attitude gauge. As much as possible, prepare yourself to stay calm. No matter what is said in the conversation, remember you are the owner of your attitude. And if someone is able to manipulate your emotions, you have given them power over you. Keep the spotlight on your goal—not on the person who may have the potential of leading you off course. Remember to fight the issue, not the person.

Bring value, not vengeance. When having a critical conversation, your goal should be to help solve the problem, not just bring an announcement that there is one.

Here are two ways I thought of to kick off the conversation:

- I would like to share some options I've been thinking about to help us reach our objectives.
- I know you've been thinking on this issue, but can I provide some ideas in respect to this situation?

You will be constantly challenged in your relationships. Problems will arise. And when they do, bring solutions and possibilities to the situation. Don't just highlight the problem.

Make sure you widen your perspective of the situation. If we're honest, we go into most conversations with our minds already made up. We make a judgment and assumptions on what we think to be true. But often we have limited information. As hard as this may be, when entering into a crucial conversation, suspend full judgment until you hear the other person's side. Yes, you know your side well and you have your own point of view, but there are always two sides to a story. Even if you don't agree, never forget to hear the other person's side.

The best way to do that is to ask questions. Now when you ask questions, don't ask questions that have a condescending or suspicious tone. I know that's hard, but try your best to give them the benefit of the doubt.

Ask questions that will help you understand the issue better.

And ask them in a sincere way to gather information and facts in order to gain a broader view of what's going on. You may not want to hear this, but your viewpoint alone is not enough to have a productive conversation.

It's important for you to see the entire picture, not just your side.

Find common ground in the conversation. No matter the situation, there is always something you can agree on. If nothing else but saying we both want to resolve this situation. Start in a place where you can both nod your head. Reassure the individual that your purpose is to positively impact the situation. Believe me, you will be able to relate better if you can agree on at least one or two common items.

Upgrade your listening skills. Whenever I'm upgraded in anything, I feel privileged and prioritized. In having a conversation with someone, upgrade your listening skills to another level. Even if you consider yourself a great listener, there's always room for improvement.

Listening conveys respect and value to the other person. And in turn, hopefully this will also communicate how you would like them to respond to you. Again, there are no guarantees how another person will respond, but you'll have a greater chance of having a productive conversation if they feel respected and valued.

TIPS FOR AFTER THE CONVERSATION.

After a conversation, you sometimes need time for things to simmer. People need time to process. So depending on who it is and where you are, give a person room to digest the conversation. When you think there has been sufficient time, go to them and follow-up. Now, this may not always be possible. But if you're able to, try it.

Here's something to remember that I learned years ago. Allow your emotions to push you forward. Use your emotions as a motivator instead of a de-motivator.

SOMETIMES YOU HAVE TO COMMUNICATE WITH SILENCE.

Well, we're at a close to this chapter. But I can't leave you without sharing some thoughts on what to do when the conversation doesn't go well.

The reality is, some people won't listen to your thoughts or ideas. And, unfortunately, it's hard to be in that kind of environment.

Sometimes one of your wisest options is to be quiet. And as you know, silence isn't always golden when you have so much you want to say. But sometimes silence is one the best actions you can take in order to navigate your challenges and to give you some degree of peace.

The fact is you are where you are for now. And although there may be unpleasant dynamics, don't allow this part of your life to become your life's focus. Fight to make sure your attitude and perspective is positive. Arm yourself heavily with a great attitude and a positive outlook. While you may be going through your trial by fire, remember the circumstances you are going through don't have to define you. And make sure you leverage the lessons you learn and use them as fuel for your relaunch.

Now as we go into this next chapter on stress, keep in mind, you only have one life to live. So don't give your sanity to anyone.

KEY# 5
CREATE HEALTHY OUTLETS TO LIFT YOUR STRESS AND KEEP YOUR SANITY

"The greatest weapon against stress is our ability to choose one thought over another."

- William James

WE'RE ALL STRESSED.

I spoke with a friend yesterday about the mounting problems and issues in her life, and at the end of the conversation she said two words that explained what she was feeling. She said, *"I'm tired"*.

Have you gotten to that point lately? Where you are so stressed out about something or someone that all you can say is, *"I'm tired?"*

No matter where you are on your journey, stress plays some role in your life. That is why I wrote this chapter last. Because I knew you would need most, if not all, of the strategies I shared in earlier chapters to help lift the load of stress in your life.

STRESS COLLIDES EVERDAY.

I've got to share this story with you as we start discussing stress.

It was a cold, rainy Friday morning and I had just dropped my kids off at school. During this time of my life, I was stressed out most days and this day was no different. Finances were still low and bill collectors were still calling.

After I dropped the kids off, I noticed the weather was getting colder by the minute. And I was, too.

So I rushed home and turned on the television to listen to the weather report. As I suspected, we were in for a winter storm...an ice storm to be exact. The weatherman gave a strong warning, "Do not go out of your home unless you have to." Then the news anchor informed everyone that the police were already overwhelmed with the number of accidents, and they were requesting that no one call the police unless someone was injured. They said you should just exchange insurance information and call in the report.

I turned off the television and headed to the school to pick up my kids. After getting my children, I realized I needed to go to the grocery store. So I dropped them off at home and left to get some food.

As I was driving, I turned down a street with a slight hill. I was barely going over five miles an hour, but the ice on the road took my van for a ride I wasn't prepared to go on. My speed began increasing. I used all of the driving skills I had, but I kept sliding. Then to my horror, I noticed a shiny black Escalade that was stopped at the red light in front of me.

I immediately prayed down heaven to please stop my van. I remember saying, "Oh God, Oh God, please don't let me hit"... and about that time my van kissed that Escalade like a long lost lover who had just returned home from war.

The driver jumped out and started screaming, explaining that this was her boss's brand new vehicle. While she was exploding with anger and saying she was going to call the police, I was exploding trying to tell her the police weren't coming. I told her all we could do was exchange insurance information and call the report in. But for ten minutes we continued exploding all over each other. It's funny to me now. But it wasn't that day.

Here is the point of this story. Not only did my vehicle collide with her vehicle. My stress collided with her stress. She was stressed because she was sent out in a brand new vehicle she didn't want to drive to pick something up in this ice storm. And I'm sure she had other things stressing her out, too. And I was stressed from my financial problems, the tension in my marriage because of them, and everything else that was going on in my life.

When was the last time your stress collided with somebody else's stress?

Our reality is that we are living in times of high stress. We see stress exhibited among drivers in road rage. We see stress in the tension in our workplace. And, unfortunately, if we are not careful, this stress rolls right into our lives and right into our homes and every other place we go. But the truth is, we don't have to live stressed-out lives. And that's what this chapter is all about. So let's take a look at stress and what we can do about it.

DO YOU KNOW YOUR WARNING SIGNS OF STRESS?

Stress is inevitable. We all know that. We are all constantly bombarded with life stressors. Some are small and some are big. But not all stress is bad. I felt stress as I neared the deadline to hand this manuscript over to my editor. But that stress helped motivate and push me to finish this book. It was positive stress.

But not all stress is positive. Being stressed out is a serious issue. The American Psychological Association says, "Stress is your body's natural reaction to any kind of demand that disrupts life as usual."

If you're not careful, stress can rob you of living a quality life. And it can even kill you if you let it.

That is why I wanted you to see the list of 50 warning signs from The American Institute of Stress*. See if you can find your warning signs?

1 Frequent headaches, jaw clenching or pain
2 Gritting, grinding teeth
3 Stuttering or stammering
4 Tremors, trembling of lips, hands
5 Neck ache, back pain, muscle spasms
6 Light headedness, faintness, dizziness
7 Ringing, buzzing or "popping sounds
8 Frequent blushing, sweating
9 Cold or sweaty hands, feet
10 Dry mouth, problems swallowing
11 Frequent colds, infections, herpes sores
12 Rashes, itching, hives, "goose bumps"
13 Unexplained or frequent "allergy" attacks
14 Heartburn, stomach pain, nausea
15 Excess belching, flatulence
16 Constipation, diarrhea, loss of control
17 Difficulty breathing, frequent sighing
18 Sudden attacks of life threatening panic
19 Chest pain, palpitations, rapid pulse
20 Frequent urination
21 Diminished sexual desire or performance
22 Excess anxiety, worry, guilt, nervousness
23 Increased anger, frustration, hostility
24 Depression, frequent or wild mood swings
25 Increased or decreased appetite
26 Insomnia, nightmares, disturbing dreams
27 Difficulty concentrating, racing thoughts
28 Trouble learning new information

29 Forgetfulness, disorganization, confusion
30 Difficulty in making decisions
31 Feeling overloaded or overwhelmed
32 Frequent crying spells or suicidal thoughts
33 Feelings of loneliness or worthlessness
34 Little interest in appearance, punctuality
35 Nervous habits, fidgeting, feet tapping
36 Increased frustration, irritability, edginess
37 Overreaction to petty annoyances
38 Increased number of minor accidents
39 Obsessive or compulsive behavior
40 Reduced work efficiency or productivity
41 Lies or excuses to cover up poor work
42 Rapid or mumbled speech
43 Excessive defensiveness or suspiciousness
44 Problems in communication, sharing
45 Social withdrawal and isolation
46 Constant tiredness, weakness, fatigue
47 Frequent use of over-the-counter drugs
48 Weight gain or loss without diet
49 Increased smoking, alcohol or drug use
50 Excessive gambling or impulse buying
    *http://www.stress.org/stress-effects/

How many of the stress signs do you have?

The reason I ask is because you need to know the signs so you know how to combat it.

One of the reasons I'm so passionate about helping people deal with stress is because I know what it can do to you if stress goes unchecked. Even as I look at that list, I can't believe how many of these issues once affected my life. I went through depression. I also gained weight and developed an ulcer. And about ten years ago I ended up in the emergency room because I thought I was having a heart attack. I later discovered, after they hooked me up to all kinds of machines and monitors, that it wasn't my heart. It was just stress. That was my wake-up call.

I'm not sure if you've had a wake-up call of any kind, but your body needs a healthy way of coping with and combating stress.

So now that we've looked at some of the symptoms of stress, let's look at some of the stressors and how they affects you.

As far back as 1967, two psychiatrists, Thomas Holmes and Richard Rahe, researched the causal link between stress and illness. What they came up with is called the (you guessed it!) Holmes and Rahe Stress Scale*. It lists life events in order of the stress levels they cause.

Below is the scale. Check to see how many of these stresses you have experienced in the past 12 months to see how high your risk is of becoming ill. The more of these stressors you have experienced, the higher your risk.

Life event	Life Change Units
Death of a spouse	100
Divorce	73
Marital separation	65
Imprisonment	63
Death of a close family member	63
Personal injury or illness	53
Marriage	50
Dismissal from work	47
Marital reconciliation	45
Retirement	45
Change in health of family member	44
Pregnancy	40
Sexual difficulties	39
Gain a new family member	39
Business readjustment	39
Change in financial state	38
Change in frequency of arguments	35
Major mortgage	32
Foreclosure of mortgage or loan	30
Change in responsibilities at work	29
Child leaving home	29
Trouble with in-laws	29
Outstanding personal achievement	28
Spouse starts or stops work	26
Begin or end school	26
Change in living conditions	25
Revision of personal habits	24
Trouble with boss	23

Change in working hours or conditions	20
Change in residence	20
Change in schools	20
Change in recreation	19
Change in church activities	19
Change in social activities	18
Minor mortgage or loan	17
Change in sleeping habits	16
Change in number of family reunions	15
Change in eating habits	15
Vacation	13
Christmas	12
Minor violation of law	11

Score of 300+: At risk of illness.

Score of 150-299+: Risk of illness is moderate (reduced by 30% from the above risk).

Score 0-150: Only has a slight risk of illness.

*http://www.health24.com/Mental-Health/Stress/Stress-management/41-major-life-stressors-20120721

What was your score?

Hopefully you're thinking about the effects stress could be having on your health right now. If you let stress go unchecked, you'll be vulnerable to all kinds of illnesses.

The American Institute of Stress reports that: *There are numerous emotional and physical disorders that have been linked to stress including depression, anxiety, heart attacks, stroke, hypertension, immune system disturbances that increase susceptibility to infections, a host of viral linked disorders ranging from the common cold and herpes to AIDS and certain cancers, as well as autoimmune diseases like rheumatoid arthritis and multiple sclerosis. In addition stress can have direct effects on the skin (rashes, hives, atopic dermatitis), the gastrointestinal system (GERD, peptic ulcer, irritable bowel syndrome, ulcerative colitis) and can contribute to insomnia and degenerative neurological disorders like Parkinson's disease. In fact, it's hard to think of any disease in which stress cannot play an aggravating role or any part of the body that is not affected....*

Do you know that the World Health Organization estimates that within the next 10 years stress-related conditions like depression will rank as the second leading cause of disability worldwide?

Listen. I know that you are probably aware that stress can be a serious issue. But thankfully there is something we all can do. We can be aware of stress signals before they affect the quality of our lives. And we can proactively counter the effects of stress. Remember this is your time to relaunch and have a personal comeback. Don't let stress stand in your way.

Let's use this chapter to look at a multitude of wise ways we can counter stress when we see it coming.

By the way, I want you to know that everything I'm going to share with you in this chapter I have personally used at different times in my relaunching journey. And I can't wait to share them with you.

But before we get started, take a few minutes to answer these questions:

How often do you feel stretched to the limit?

- What triggers can you create to alert yourself to the fact that you're getting stressed out?
- How much time do you allot for taking breaks to relax and rest during the day?
- What is your favorite way to spend some downtime?
- What is preventing you from having more downtime?
- How do you feel about devoting more time to yourself?
- Describe how you feel after you have experienced some downtime?
- What adjustments can you make to your schedule to include more downtime?

IDENTIFY WHAT IS STRESSING YOU OUT THE MOST.

I know we looked at a list earlier, but I wanted to share some comments I have heard from many people concerning their stress.

Work-related stress

"I'm so busy at work that sometimes I skip lunch."
"I'm only staying at my job for the money."
"Everyone thinks I have a great job. If they only knew."

Lack of finances

"I have more bills than my budget can afford."

"I'm working and I still don't have money for myself."
"When will I ever get ahead?"

Being too busy
" I feel like I can never catch up."

I bet you can probably relate to that last statement.

Last week I was in a friend's office as she was packing up her laptop and several documents from her desk. She was talking to me and preparing to run out the door to another appointment. As she was busy getting ready to leave I heard her murmur these words, *"I feel like I can never catch up."*

Isn't that the mantra of most people? We've all felt that way at some point. But the problem is most of us feel that way right now.

I remember one day several years ago, I was busy running errands for different people. Out of the blue I said to myself, *"I feel like everybody's mother."*

I knew when I said those words that it was a sign I was exhausted and overwhelmed. Sometimes words will come out of you that you don't expect and that tell you something you need to pay attention to.

Has that happened to you lately?

Whenever words like these flow out of you, I believe it's a warning you need to slow down. Even unconsciously we will utter words that reveal we are beyond tired. And most of the time, beyond stressed.

This is what I know. If you want to relaunch, you will have to lighten your load of stress.

So let's look at how to do that.

LEAVE THE OVERWHELMED LIFE BEHIND.

I know what stress can do to a person. I almost went insane. I tell people all the time when I describe my depression days, I was keeping everybody together while I was falling apart.

That's why I won't allow being overwhelmed to be the theme of my life anymore. And I know you won't either. That's why you're reading this book.

We've all experienced the overloaded life. And we all know how it plays itself out.

The average day is packed to capacity with things to do. The assembly line of daily demands and deadlines just keeps rolling out. Emails, texts and phone calls just add more moving pieces and parts to work and life responsibilities. Not to mention all the additional tasks people ask us to do.

Think about it. Most of us kick-start our day with more on our to-do list than we have time for. Then at the end of the day, we are tired from what we did and frustrated about what we didn't get done. Then the next day we wake up again to all the leftover responsibilities. And we're even more stressed out trying to figure out how in the world we're going to be able to get everything done.

Unfortunately, in today's world it's normal and accepted to be exhausted from a packed schedule.

But we do have a choice. We don't have to live like this. We can stop the madness. Being overwhelmed is a recipe for all kinds of mental and emotional ruts.

Time out!

As a depression survivor for almost fifteen years now, I'm still using the stress-less strategies I share with you in this chapter.

The less stressed you are, the greater your chance of relaunching.

So here's what you should do.

PUT "YOU" ON YOUR SCHEDULE.

I was just talking to a mom the other day about mommy guilt. That guilt many mothers feel when they do something for themselves without their children. My children are grown now, but when they were younger, I experienced mommy guilt. But I also spent many years in depression. It was after the depression that I realized part of it came about because I didn't prioritize me on my schedule.

Maybe you don't deal with mommy guilt. Maybe you feel guilty for not doing more with your family or friends. Now I'm not saying you shouldn't spend time with other people and do certain things. But if you don't prioritize you on your schedule, who will?

If you're having a tough time on your job, in a relationship or dealing with stress in any area of your life, you especially need to make time for you. You need time just to think and process what's going on and what your next move will be. You need time to just enjoy you and the benefits of being alone.

As I look back on my business failure, I never took the time to get away while I was operating my business. I thought success required me to put in long hours. I didn't realize that recipe for success also included the potential of getting in a rut.

I made little time for me before, during and after the business. So when I transitioned and switched hats and became an employee, I just plunged ahead with my same destructive patterns.

This is what I've discovered. No one can function in a healthy way without proper breaks. Something has to give.

Think about it. What has the payoff been for having an overwhelming schedule?

Just look around at all the overwhelmed people you know. How many of them are living optimal lives?

Do you see where I'm going with this? If you haven't already, it's time to put you on your schedule.

So where do you start?

The first place to start is to become time sensitive.

BECOME TIME-SENSITIVE.

I received an email the other day with the words *time sensitive* in the subject line. I opened it up because I knew it was important. Those words meant I should prioritize that email. It also meant there was an approaching deadline. And it also told me I had a short window to make a decision.

The bottom line was I knew I couldn't waste time opening and responding to that email. It was a call to action. Similarly, your life, your existence, your every breath has a stamp on it. Time sensitive.

You can't stop the clock, but you can guard your time.

PUT A LIMIT ON HOW MANY PEOPLE YOU CAN HELP.

"Can I ask you a favor?"

When was the last time you were asked that question? How did you respond?

Here's the truth and you know it: Everybody around you has needs. And for some reason you're probably the person they like to call on. And if that's the case, you'll need a strategy to determine which situations and people to say *yes* to and which ones to say *no* to. I will tell you that I have learned to say no more in the last few years than ever before in my life.

Frankly, if you want to make the most of your time, saying "no" has to be a part of your lifestyle. Now saying no can be done in a variety of ways, but however you do it you can be nice and still own your time. I do believe we should help others, but not everybody. You should assess each request and the person asking. Why? To make sure you're being wise with your time and also to make sure you're not being taken advantage of.

There have been times when people have asked me for a favor and it was simply because they hadn't been responsible with their time, money, or priorities. And when they called me, they were in crisis mode and needed me to rescue them. And many times I have had to say no.

This may sound harsh, but you must guard your time.

Just last night I was checking Facebook, which I only do at night once I have completed all the essential activities I needed to do that day. As I was looking at my page, a message popped up from a sweet lady asking me to please listen to a conference call to help her with her business. I only said yes because she said it would only take twenty minutes.

But I regretted it later because I knew better. I should have asked questions to assess whether or not this was something I should be investing my time in. I had gotten caught up in the fact that she's a nice lady.

Well, I made the call.

And after listening for a few minutes, I realized that it was a call to recruit me into her business. I hung up the phone and immediately sent her a very short message sharing with her that the business was not for me. And also that I have a business myself. That was all I wrote in the message. I didn't go into a full explanation about my busy schedule. It wasn't necessary. I didn't have to apologize for having a life.

I thought that would be sufficient. It was a nice message, but ultimately I said no.

Obviously that message didn't take. She responded asking me to consider being in the business so she could meet her goals. She then offered me the opportunity to get products at half price. She didn't seem to consider that I have my own business and my own goals in that business.

At the end of the day, it really doesn't matter whether or not she or anyone else values my time and my goals. What matters is that I prioritize my time and not get sidetracked. I have a responsibility for my time and what I do with it. Time is too precious to be wasted.

Here's my point. People are more in tune to their own life and their goals. And that's fine. Just make sure you're in tune to yours, too.

TRY THESE DE-STRESSORS TO HELP REFRESH, RESET AND RELAUNCH.

With everything that's going on in your life, you need to de-stress and decompress every day. Don't wait until you feel like you need it. It's wise to incorporate de-stress strategies into every day. Even when you don't feel stress, it's a part of our lives. So here is a list of my favorite ways to get past stress. Listen, this list isn't inclusive of every idea to reduce stress. So use what fits you and add your favorites to the list. Just do something to take control of your stress.

Start your day with inspiration. How you start your day is important. The beginning of your day sets the tone for the entire day. Become very intentional with what you allow in your mind in the morning. Don't let just any message sink in. Determine the most inspiring way to shape your thoughts for the day. For me, I love to pray and meditate. It sets the tone I want and gives me peace knowing I'm not doing life on my own.

Take an inspirational break. Find something inspiring to think about that lifts your spirit. For me, I keep a note card with a quote, a Bible verse or an inspirational message on it to think about throughout the day. Or sometimes I will listen to something motivational or inspirational. Or I'll read something that stirs my heart to want to live a greater life.

Unwind daily. Make time in your busy schedule to exhale with something relaxing at the end of the day. Especially after a hard day of work you need to decompress. Try a hot bubble bath. Or watch sports or a favorite television program. Do whatever helps you release the pressure of the day.

Plan a get-away. If you can't afford a luxurious vacation, take a visit to a relative's house that's out of town. Just the fact that you are changing scenery in your life for a few days is a mood lifter. When was the last time you got away?

Fresh Air Fiesta. A friend came to my house after work for a meeting. She arrived early and was obviously stressed out from something on her job. I asked her if she wanted to talk. She surprised me when she said, "No, I need to take a walk." She was in no mood to be bombarded with questions. She quickly changed clothes and walked around a nearby track for about thirty minutes. I noticed how her disposition had changed the minute she walked back in the house. Her problem clearly hadn't gone away. But she felt better releasing some of the tension and allowing herself to critically think through her next move.

Make laughter a part of your life. When was the last time you had a good laugh? How did you feel? A good dose of laughter can take the edge off of stress and release endorphins. Just infusing humor into your life has the ability to relieve tension and lift your spirits. Need a lift in life? Have a good laugh as often as you can.

Eat healthy. I know you are fully aware of this message. We all are. So as tempting as it may be to turn to the sugary and fatty foods, be prepared with some alternatives. Keep fruits and vegetables handy to grab and eat.

Exercise. There are all kinds of exercise you can do. But I've found a secret to exercising. Don't do what you hate. Do what you love and you won't stop doing it. So fit the exercise you love into your daily schedule.

More suggestions to decrease stress:

- Try deep breathing exercises.
- Get enough rest and sleep.
- Get professional help.
- Keep a journal.
- Stop complaining.
- Accept some things you cannot change.
- Listen to calming music.
- Get a massage.
- Give yourself extra time to get where you're going.
- Enjoy a good cry.

FINALLY...

As you've read this chapter, I'm sure you already knew some of what I wrote. But it's not what you know that makes the difference in your life. It's what you do with what you know that changes your life. So my friend, as we end our time together, my hope is that you'll make a full commitment to decrease your stress and to take relentless action to make your great relaunch a reality.

CONCLUSION

IT HAPPENED! BUT YOU CAN RELAUNCH!

One of the hardest parts of writing a book is deciding where to start and where to finish. So I guess I'll end with the same thought I started with. *You can relaunch right where you are.*

I hope you believe that now.

Because at the end of the day, you have one life to live. Determine with everything in you to live it well.

So whatever your story, don't get stuck in it.

I know as well as anyone what a waste that is.

My story left me stuck. But one day I realized I wanted to live a different one. I wanted my children and the world to know that when your story hits the painful spots, when your life and circumstances ground you, with the right strategies and the right tools—you can relaunch.

So whatever your "it" is that has caused you to be stressed out or stuck, my question for you is: Are you ready to change your story?

My friend, there will be days when it will be hard to keep yourself fired up. There will be days when you won't feel like doing a dog-gone thing. And on those days, you'll have to fight harder to feed your mind, your body, and your spirit. But on those days, don't you dare stop. Don't you throw out your dreams, desires, and goals. Don't throw out your growth plan. Examine it. Modify it, if necessary. But don't give up on getting past stuck and stress. Just get ready for another day and another fight.

This is your time to relaunch! Go live the story you want to tell!

ACKNOWLEDGMENTS

Rhonda J. Fleming, my editor and friend, thank you for helping bring this book to life. Your expertise, experience and encouragement fueled me throughout this project.

Antwala Robinson, my friend and comrade in arms, your accountability, laughter and listening ear kept me focused through this project.

Nanette Taylor, my friend, you believed in me before I ever wrote my first words.

Dexter, my husband and best friend in all the world, you saw the best in me when I couldn't see it in myself. I love being your partner for life.

Danielle, Philip, Monica and Jasmine, my beautiful children, thank you for all the time you gave me to write this book and the many times you texted and called to say you were proud of me.

And last, but never least, my Lord and Savior, Jesus Christ, without Him this book would have never been written.

ABOUT THE AUTHOR

Kim Hardy is an author, national speaker and coach who has the ability to inspire individuals to embrace positive change.

A seasoned speaker, Kim has presented over 500 keynotes and seminars from churches to corporations to educational entities. She is one of a handful of professional speakers that delivers high-energy, high-content presentations that educate, equip and entertain.

She is the author of six books and continues to write the messages that burn within her heart.

One of her deepest desires is to help others find and live out their purpose and passions in life.

She makes her home in Georgia, with her husband, her mom, and the youngest of their four children.

Kim welcomes the opportunity to speak at your next event, seminar, or conference. She can be contacted at Kimhardyspeaks.com.

Feel free to send your thoughts and comments.

Volume discounts are available.